GENDER IDENTITY WORKBOOK FOR TEENS

GENDER IDENTITY
WORKBOOK
for

TEENS

Practical Exercises to
Navigate Your Exploration,
Support Your Journey, and
Celebrate Who You Are

Andrew Maxwell Triska, LCSW

Illustrations by Ana Jaks

callisto
publishing
an imprint of Sourcebooks

Published by Callisto Publishing LLC C/O Sourcebooks LLC
P.O. Box 4410, Naperville, Illinois 60567-4410
(630) 961-3900
callistopublishing.com

Printed and bound in China
WKT 2

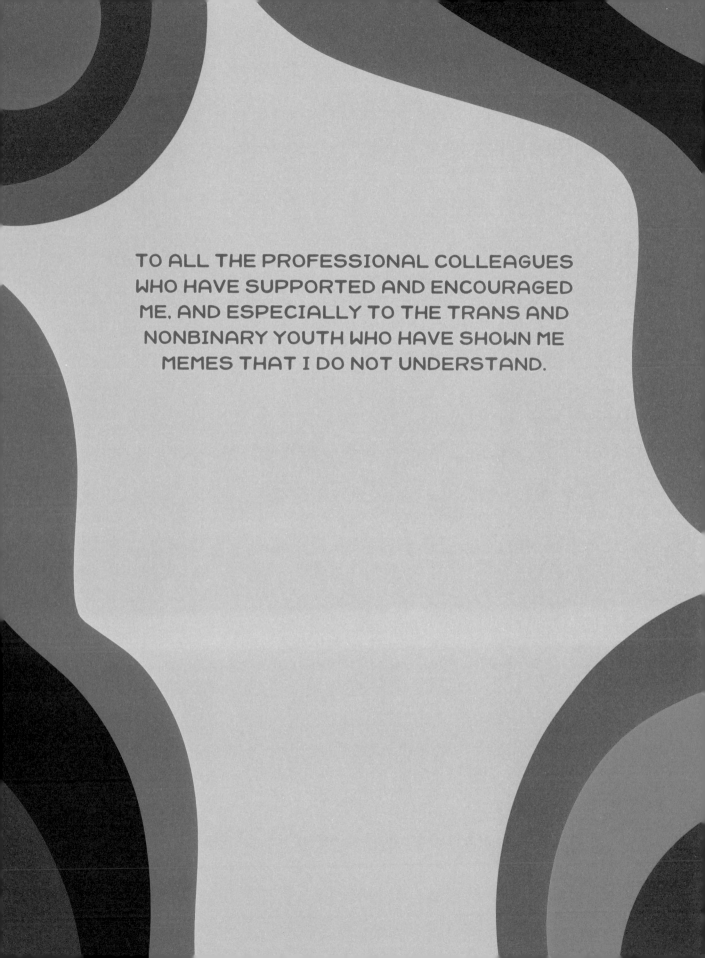

TO ALL THE PROFESSIONAL COLLEAGUES WHO HAVE SUPPORTED AND ENCOURAGED ME, AND ESPECIALLY TO THE TRANS AND NONBINARY YOUTH WHO HAVE SHOWN ME MEMES THAT I DO NOT UNDERSTAND.

CONTENTS

INTRODUCTION

Welcome to the *Gender Identity Workbook for Teens*. This workbook is designed to help you explore your gender identity and find out more about who you are and who you want to be. You might have picked it up because you've been having thoughts and feelings that are making you ask tough questions about your gender. Or maybe you're just a bit curious about yourself. No matter the reason, you've found your way to it.

Gender is complicated, and questioning your gender can cause other questions and worries to pop up: *What do I do if I realize I'm trans? How do I tell my family? How do I really know who I am? What if I'm not who I thought I was?*

Maybe you picked up this workbook hoping it would answer some of these questions. Do any of these sound like you, or like versions of questions you've wondered about yourself?

→ "I've never felt like a girl. My parents call me a tomboy. But it's not like I want to *do* guy things—I think I *am* a guy. I don't think they'll understand if I tell them that. What do I do?"

→ "I think I might be trans, but I don't know if I want to change my body physically. Can you be trans but not want hormones or surgery?"

→ "My family is okay with me wearing girls' clothes and using she/her pronouns, but I know my best friend is going to think I'm weird if I show up to his house in a skirt. How do I get him to understand that this is who I am?"

→ "I'm happy being a guy, but I have more of a feminine style and want to start wearing makeup outside my house. I go to a Catholic school and worry how it would go over there. How am I going to express myself and not get sent home?"

→ "Other trans people on the internet tell me that I need to come out, but I'm happy keeping it to myself for now. Is there anything wrong with that?"

This workbook will help you answer questions like these and many more. But don't think that exploring your identity is going to be all about worrying, because you're sure to have positive feelings, too. Maybe you'll feel a flash of recognition reading about other people's experiences or start to feel more comfortable expressing yourself to your family or classmates. Or maybe you'll feel relieved that there are words for the things you're feeling *right now*.

As a therapist, I've worked with teens across the gender spectrum who came to therapy to learn more about themselves and sometimes to make important life changes. Although it isn't a substitute for therapy, this interactive workbook might help you prepare to talk to a therapist about what you're experiencing right now. It will take you through the process of exploring your gender step-by-step using broad, real-world examples based on clients I've worked with, people I've known in real life, historical trans pioneers, and my own gender journey. You may not feel 100 percent sure of your gender identity at the end, and that's okay. But once we've finished, you'll have some insight into your feelings around your gender, and you'll have a better understanding of how to assert yourself, communicate your needs, and be more prepared to engage with your world in a genuine way.

In part 1, we'll begin by exploring the basic building blocks of gender: the social, physical, and psychological parts that compose your gender identity. In part 2, you'll work through activities and exercises that will help you answer important questions about your brain, body, emotions, and a lot more. In part 3, we'll explore practical tools and tips to help you with the everyday challenges you might face in becoming your true self.

Let's get started!

PART 1

EXPLORING THE GENDER SPECTRUM: A WORLD OF POSSIBILITIES

Before we start this trip, we'll need an accurate map to guide us. The language we use to describe gender identity is constantly changing as we refine what we know already, research the workings of the human brain, and gain a better understanding of the ways different people and cultures relate to gender. In the first section, we'll discuss the words we use when we talk about gender.

WHAT IS GENDER IDENTITY?

Your *gender identity* is made up of a lot of things. One big part of gender identity is your inner sense: your deep-down feelings about whether you're male or female or identify outside of the gender binary. Gender identity can also include your feelings about your body and your social self. You might feel the need for your body to look a certain way or want to change some things about it. Maybe it's important to you that other people see you a certain way. No matter how you feel, it's normal for some of these things to be more important to you than others or for some not to be important at all.

Some people find it helpful to think of gender identity as a spectrum or scale, with *male* on one end and *female* on the other. You might place yourself on one of the far ends of the spectrum, right in the middle, or more to one side. However, it's possible that a spectrum with just two labels doesn't describe your gender identity at all. We'll talk more about the gender spectrum later and explore other ways of thinking about it, too.

When you hear *gender identity*, you might picture the way people express their gender outwardly, with clothing, makeup, hairstyles, and the way they walk and talk. We call these signs *gender expression*. They're the ways someone shows masculinity or femininity, whether it's with a flannel shirt and jeans or high heels and painted nails (or a flannel shirt and painted nails). Your gender expression can be a *part* of your gender identity, but it definitely isn't *all* of it. Two people might have the same clothes and haircut but describe their genders in completely different ways.

Your gender identity is also different from your *gender role*, or the way you're expected to think and act based on your gender. How often do you see male characters in TV shows or movies caring for others or expressing feelings in a gentle way, without anger? Do female characters have major story lines that are funny, scary, or tragic like the male characters, or do they exist just to fight with each other about guys? Those are all gender roles at work. But the way you relate to your gender role doesn't have to match your gender identity. Just because you cry easily or have "manly" hobbies doesn't mean that your gender identity isn't real or that you can't apply a label you feel is a good fit with who you are.

Hearing *gender identity* might make you think of the word *transgender*. People usually use that label when there's a difference between the identification *male* or *female* on their birth certificate (sometimes called *assigned gender*) and their gender identity. It applies to many people who use many different labels. Not everyone who doesn't identify with their assigned gender uses the word *transgender*, and you don't have to be transgender, or any other identity, to use this workbook.

You might think of pronouns, too—words like *he*, *she*, *they*, or *ze* that refer to people in the third person. You can't necessarily tell someone's identity by the pronouns they use, and not everyone with the same identity uses the same pronouns; three different nonbinary people might use he, she, and they. In this workbook, we'll use *they* to refer to people whose gender isn't specified.

Finally, your gender identity isn't the same as your *sexual orientation*, which is what we call your sexual and romantic attractions—or lack of attraction, if you're asexual or aromantic (meaning you don't have sexual feelings or romantic desires). These attractions don't imply anything about your gender identity (for example, being attracted to women doesn't make you a man). However, you might find that you feel more confident exploring your sexuality when you're more comfortable with your body and able to express your gender identity fully.

A CLOSER LOOK AT DIFFERENT IDENTITIES

Before we go any further, we're going to talk about different labels that people apply to themselves and how they can change over time. You might find that one or more of these labels describes you perfectly, that none are a good fit, or that you might not be comfortable using *any* label right now. That's all a normal part of your gender journey.

You'll notice that a lot of these labels are similar or overlap. That's because there's no single authority on gender and language! Different people, cultures, and movements have come up with many terms over the years to describe themselves. You might even know a few descriptions that aren't in this workbook.

Agender or Genderless

Agender or **genderless** describes someone who doesn't feel like they have *any* gender, which is different from feeling like you're somewhere between male and female or a mix of the two. An agender or genderless person might also feel that gender is unimportant to their identity or that the male-female gender spectrum doesn't apply to them.

Androgyne

Androgyne is a term for someone whose gender identity or expression is androgynous; in other words, it's a mix of male and female, or masculine and feminine.

Binary

Someone who identifies as **binary** places themself on one of the two ends of the male-female gender spectrum. A *binary male*, for example, is someone whose identity doesn't have any female elements. He's a guy.

Butch

Butch is a word that some people with a masculine gender expression use to describe themselves. It is most often used by lesbians but can be used by anyone.

Cisgender

Cisgender describes someone who identifies with the gender assigned to them at birth. For example, if there's an *M* on your birth certificate and you fully identify as male, you're cisgender.

Cross-dresser

A **cross-dresser** is someone who wears clothes that aren't usually worn by people of their gender. Usually, people use this word to describe men who dress like women in public or private, either because they're more comfortable in those clothes or because it feels exciting. However, most people who dress in nontraditional clothing don't call themselves cross-dressers. Lots of women prefer to shop in the men's section of a clothing store, and lots of men wear makeup and skirts without using this label. Drag queens/kings also don't usually call themselves cross-dressers. Although many people use this word as a self-descriptor, it's disrespectful to apply this term to anyone who doesn't use it themselves, since it's often used to insult or degrade gender variant people.

Demigender

Demigender describes someone who identifies partially, but not completely, with one binary gender. For example, a **demigirl** is someone who identifies as more female, while a **demiboy** identifies as more male.

Drag

A **drag queen** or **drag king** is someone who performs as a woman or a man, often in a pageant or nightclub, usually taking on a larger-than-life persona. Drag queens and kings use their personas' pronouns while in drag and their own pronouns when they're not. Being in drag is not the same as being transgender, though many drag queens and kings are also transgender or gender variant.

Femme

Femme describes someone whose gender expression tends toward the traditionally feminine end of the gender spectrum.

Gender/Sex Assigned at Birth

Gender/sex assigned at birth, sometimes called **birth gender/sex**, refers to the *M* or *F* on your birth certificate. Some people use abbreviations like AFAB or AMAB, which stand for "assigned female/male at birth." "Gender assigned at birth" is the more accurate and preferred term, since most gender variant people feel they have always been their identified gender, even if their birth certificate doesn't say so.

Gender Dysphoria

Gender dysphoria is a feeling of unhappiness or discomfort with your assigned gender. Dysphoria can be with your body (like your chest), your social role (like your name and pronouns), or your gender expression (like your hair length). Not every trans or nonbinary person uses the word *dysphoria* to describe their experiences. The opposite term is **gender euphoria**: a feeling of happiness or comfort that comes from affirming your identity.

Gender Expansive/Gender Diverse/Gender Variant

Gender expansive, **gender diverse**, and **gender variant** are terms that cover anyone whose gender identity or expression doesn't fit with the norm, including identities like transgender, nonbinary, and most other identity labels. We'll be using *gender variant* in this workbook regularly as a catchall term.

Genderfluid

Genderfluid means having a gender identity that shifts over time. A genderfluid person might feel more like a boy at one time and more like a girl a few hours, days, or weeks later. Or they might express aspects of different genders at the same time.

Genderqueer

Genderqueer is a label people use when they have a gender identity or expression that differs from the norm for their assigned gender—hence the word *queer*, which can mean "different" or "outside the ordinary." Sometimes, people who are genderqueer also identify as transgender, nonbinary, agender, or another label. A similar term is **gender nonconforming**, which refers to someone with a gender *expression* (but not always a gender *identity*) that differs from the norm.

Identified Gender

Identified gender is your actual gender: the gender you feel you are inside, regardless of what the doctor labeled you when you were born. A cisgender person's identified gender and gender assigned at birth are the same, while a transgender person's are different.

Masc

Masc describes someone whose gender identity or expression tends toward the masculine end of the gender spectrum.

Nonbinary/Enby

Nonbinary (sometimes shortened to **enby**) is a broad term for any gender identity outside the binary of male and female. Identities that fall under this umbrella include agender, genderqueer, androgyne, and genderfluid. Some people just call themselves nonbinary while others use more than one word to describe themselves. Someone who identifies more toward the female end of the gender spectrum, for example, might use the label *nonbinary woman*.

Transgender/Trans

Transgender refers to someone who does not identify with the gender assigned to them at birth. Some people shorten it to **trans**. A trans person may identify with a binary gender (a *trans man/male* or *trans woman/female*) or as nonbinary, genderqueer, or something else. *Transsexual* used to be widely used to describe people who don't identify with their birth gender and want to transition (take social or physical steps to live as their identified gender), but that term isn't used much anymore, and some people consider it offensive.

Transfeminine/Transmasculine

A **transfeminine** person was assigned male at birth and has a gender identity and/or expression that tends toward the female, or feminine, end of the spectrum. **Transmasculine** describes someone who was assigned female at birth but whose gender identity and/or expression tends more toward the male, or masculine, end of the gender spectrum. Some people shorten the term to **transfem/transmasc**.

GENDER, SEX, AND OTHER WEIRD WORDS

If you've ever had a conversation with someone about gender, you might have heard phrases like "gender is different from sex." But what are we talking about when we say words like *gender* and *sex*, and what does biology have to do with it?

Usually, when people use the word *sex*, they mean "biological sex," and they're talking about DNA and the outward characteristics that make the doctor say, "It's a boy!" or "It's a girl!" when a baby is born. Biologists call this *sex differentiation*.

However, sex differentiation is complicated. Your chromosomes, hormones, and body shape don't always tell the full story. *Intersex* people, for example, are born with the characteristics of both sexes due to genetic or hormonal differences and often have bodies that don't fit typical male or female standards. Research on the brains of trans people has also shown characteristics more similar to those of cis people of their identified gender, which some scientists believe is the result of genetics, hormone exposure prebirth, or other factors.

So where does your biological sex live? In your chromosomes? Your brain? Your body parts? It's becoming clearer that *biological sex* isn't a very useful term when we're talking about gender variant people. Sure, it's important for your doctor to know what body parts you have, but your body's physical makeup isn't at all important when we're talking about how you should live, what you should wear, and what you call yourself.

Since we don't know exactly where gender comes from, we also don't know exactly where *gender variance* (differences in gender) comes from, though it's likely a mix of biological and social factors and may differ from person to person. However, we do know from decades of research—and from thousands of personal stories from gender variant people—that when people are able to live as their identified gender, they're happier. We don't need brain scans to know that people should be allowed to make decisions about their own bodies and lives.

Your physical appearance makes up part of your gender, but gender is also about less obvious things, like inner identity and social roles. Many characteristics associated with gender are based on social roles, not identity or biology, and they change over time. In 18th-century France, for instance, it was common for both men and women to wear fancy wigs, makeup, and colorful clothes.

When you begin to explore your gender, you might start questioning one or all of these things. Maybe you'll do some deep thinking and start listening to what your brain is telling you about your identity. Maybe you'll pick up a hobby you were afraid to try before because it didn't match the gender role you thought you were supposed to fit into. Or maybe you'll experiment with changing your appearance to match your identity. All of these are part of your journey!

Gender Exploration versus Gender Transitioning

You might have noticed the word *explore* keeps coming up. Why? Because it's normal to explore—and experiment with—your gender to see what fits. One person might start wearing a chest binder to see if having a flat chest makes them feel more comfortable with their body. Another person might try voice training to make their voice higher and softer. Gender exploration can be public, like going by a new name, or private, like doing your makeup when your parents aren't home.

But exploring gender isn't the same as transitioning. You don't have to commit to an identity or make physical changes to see whether something feels right. Even if part of your gender exploration is public, it doesn't mean you have to announce your gender identity to the world, especially if you're not sure yet. If people ask questions, you can simply say, "I'm trying something new"—you're not required to give an explanation. Remember, it's okay to set boundaries around *what* you tell people and *who* you tell. No one has the right to know every detail about your identity, body, or medical history.

Gender Identity Trailblazer: Andrea Jenkins (1961–)

Andrea Jenkins is the first openly transgender Black woman to be elected to public office in the United States. An artist, writer, and activist, Jenkins grew up in Chicago and holds two master's degrees. In 2015, she launched a sweeping oral history project at the University of Minnesota, recording hundreds of hours of interviews with trans and gender-nonconforming people, including those often ignored by historians, like elders and people of color. Since 2018, she has served as the vice president of the Minneapolis City Council, focusing on such issues as racial equity, public transportation, and affordable housing.

LIVING IN YOUR BODY

Some people will tell you that you have to like your body all the time, and you may have heard phrases like "be positive" or "love your flaws." If you hear enough messages like these, you might notice yourself brushing away your own feelings about your body and thinking thoughts like "I shouldn't feel this way. I'm not being a good supporter of people with bodies like mine."

However, it's important to let yourself feel those feelings rather than telling yourself that the way you feel is wrong. No one can see inside your head, and no one has the right to tell you to love your hips or think 100 percent positive thoughts about your face, butt, or stomach. Wanting to change parts of your body, or not feeling good about all of your body, isn't the same as hating your body or yourself.

But if you're constantly comparing your body to other bodies, it might be a good idea to check in with yourself about your body image. Do you feel bad because you're worried other people might not find you attractive, even if *you* like the way you look? Do you feel worse when you look at people's bodies in ads or on TV? Are there parts of your body you liked until someone criticized them?

If any of those things are true, you might want to make an effort to change your habits and what you focus on—the magazines you read, the people you follow on social media, or the way you talk and think about other people's bodies. If you follow a lot of models or influencers on Instagram, for example, pay attention to how that's affecting the way you look at yourself. Unfollow anyone who consistently makes your day worse by stirring up your negative self-talk. If you find your friends are always talking about people's looks—who gained weight this summer, whose acne got worse—think about whether this is making you and others self-conscious about body differences that wouldn't be important otherwise.

Many gender variant teens wonder whether liking their bodies, or parts of their bodies, makes their identities less real. But being gender variant isn't about feeling bad about yourself. You can like your body and still want to change it. Or you can feel fine about the way your body looks and not want to make any physical changes. None of this has an effect on what you're allowed to call yourself or whether your gender identity is authentic.

MY GENDER CHECK-IN

All of this gender information might seem a little confusing. You might be struggling to figure out which parts of gender are hardwired into your brain and which ones are shaped by the expectations of the people and society around you. If you come from a culture with firm views about gender, you may have deeply rooted beliefs about gender roles that are tough to untangle.

Let's try a quiz. Read each pair of statements and circle the one that best fits your feelings about gender roles. Try to answer honestly, even if you don't think your choice sounds like the "right" answer. There are no wrong answers in this quiz!

A	B
I have a lot of trouble understanding why someone with a male identity would ever want to wear a dress.	It's easy to see why a man might wear feminine clothing, whether he's cis or trans.
I think men naturally want to do physical jobs, like construction or firefighting.	A lot of factors go into how men choose jobs—like having male role models with that job or being encouraged by teachers and parents.
Sometimes I feel uncomfortable when I meet a woman who is quite masculine. I don't *want* to feel uncomfortable—I just do.	I have women in my family and friend group who are masculine, feminine, and in between.
Biology explains everything about the differences between men and women, physical and social.	Biology explains some things, but many of the differences people think are biological are actually learned behavior.
Girls naturally want to wear cute clothes and makeup—it's in their genes.	The clothes and makeup that girls are expected to wear have changed a lot throughout history.
I would feel embarrassed if I went out of the house in clothing that isn't usual for someone of my gender.	I'd feel okay experimenting with my gender expression through my clothing.

A	B
Women are gifted at caring for others.	Women are often expected to take on caregiving roles. Some are comfortable with these roles, while others wish they didn't have to take them on.
I don't see how you can be nonbinary. You're either one or the other.	Everyone's identity is made up of a lot of factors. Even if I don't understand someone's identity, I know that there must be important feelings behind it.
Guys are better at video games because they have better hand-eye coordination. Girls usually game because their boyfriends introduced them to it.	Anyone can be good at video games. But it's a lot more socially acceptable for men to play. Women who game sometimes quit because they get harassed online.

If you circled more column A statements: You may have some fixed ideas about gender roles that are holding you back from figuring out who you are. You could find yourself resisting doing things you've always wanted to do—maybe because they don't seem to fit the gender assigned to you at birth or don't match your identified gender. You may ask yourself questions like "Can I really be X identity if I like Y? Can someone who enjoys A have a gender identity that's B?" This is totally normal. Not everyone grows up in a family or environment that's open to gender behavior outside the norm. But you might want to be open to questioning some of these beliefs. That's what this workbook is for!

If you circled more column B statements: You probably have flexible ideas about gender roles. You realize that many of the things we do, say, and wear are based on social rules, not baked into our brains. You try not to let these rules keep you from enjoying the things you enjoy, even if other people aren't always okay with it.

Now, with the next exercise, let's do some thinking about your own identity. On the one hand, you might be totally open to all the possibilities of your gender identity. On the other hand, you might have the tendency to dismiss your own feelings or compare yourself to others in ways that aren't helpful. This can be a roadblock to self-exploration. After all, it's hard to come to conclusions about your identity if you don't trust yourself to know who you are and what you want.

Check any of the following items that match something you've felt about yourself lately.

- ☐ 1. Some of the thoughts I've been having about my gender identity are unacceptable to me.

- ☐ 2. I can't always put into words what I'm feeling about my gender, but I know these feelings are important.

- ☐ 3. I don't feel like I could be gender variant because I'm not exactly like other gender variant people I know.

- ☐ 4. I'm feeling hopeful about figuring myself out.

- ☐ 5. I don't think the thoughts I have about my body are normal—even for gender variant people. This bothers me.

- ☐ 6. I think my identity should be celebrated!

- ☐ 7. I sometimes think I shouldn't pay attention to my feelings about my gender identity because they seem strange or silly.

- ☐ 8. I think I can accept my gender identity.

- ☐ 9. I would be so embarrassed if people could see into my head right now.

- ☐ 10. My identity is valid even if no one else accepts it.

- ☐ 11. I feel like if I claimed a certain gender identity, I'd be a phony, even if that identity felt right to me.

- ☐ 12. If I've been having strong feelings about something for a long time, it must be important.

- ☐ 13. I don't feel like I have the right to waste anyone's time talking about my gender identity.

- ☐ 14. I need to listen to myself more. I'm the expert on what I want.

- ☐ 15. I constantly question everything. Sometimes I wonder if I second-guess myself too much.

If you checked more odd-numbered items: You might be struggling with self-acceptance by constantly telling yourself that your feelings about gender identity should be ignored or don't matter. Maybe you grew up in a culture where certain feelings were considered shameful. Maybe you have fixed ideas about what a "real" gender variant person is, and you don't think you fit that mold. Or maybe the people around you are always second-guessing you and you've started to second-guess yourself, too. Try to remember that if a feeling or thought is affecting your life in a real way, it's worth taking seriously. Judging or criticizing yourself when you're not hurting anyone is rarely helpful.

If you checked more even-numbered items: You're probably coming into your gender journey with an open mind about what you might find out along the way. You know that your feelings about your gender are valid no matter whether anyone else recognizes them. You know that your thoughts are worthwhile and should be taken seriously. Overall, you're good at listening to yourself. That's going to come in handy as you go through this workbook.

If you checked about the same number of even and odd items: You're probably right on the edge of self-acceptance. However, you might also be allowing doubts to make you question whether your gender identity is even worth exploring. It might be time to ask yourself, "What would I lose by paying more attention to the voice that says *take yourself seriously* than the one that says *you don't deserve to be taken seriously*?" Is your inner voice helping you or holding you back? Keep these questions in mind as you go through the rest of this workbook.

Being Your Own Best Champion

Speaking up about your needs can be tough, especially if other people make your concerns seem less significant than they are. But it's important to be your own best champion whenever you can.

Raúl's Story

Even though Raúl told his teachers about his transition, they still called him "she" and used the wrong name. It was hard for him to speak up because he felt like if he said anything, he'd just draw more attention. The situation made him want to stay quiet in class even when he had something to say. Raúl talked with the principal, but she didn't seem to understand. "At least they're trying," she said. "You need to be patient." It was so frustrating! The students got his pronouns right—why couldn't the teachers?

Raúl decided that he needed a supporter and went to the school counselor. The counselor agreed to meet with Raúl's teachers and help them understand why Raúl's correct name and pronouns were important to him. Raúl and the counselor practiced what to say if a teacher used the wrong name or pronoun. This helped Raúl feel more confident speaking up when it happened.

Raúl was glad he'd reached out for help—not just because the counselor had helped him but also because it was good to hear he wasn't doing anything wrong by speaking up. *Sometimes, having the right person in your corner can make a big difference.*

Emmie's Story

Emmie decided it was finally time to learn how to swim. They showed up to swim class the first day wearing board shorts and a cute purple swim top. But their swim instructor took them aside and told them to go change. Because Emmie was assigned male at birth, the swim instructor didn't think their top was appropriate. Emmie tried to explain that they were nonbinary and didn't feel comfortable swimming with a bare chest, but the instructor cut them off: "Whatever. Go change." Emmie felt they had no choice.

Emmie's parents were worried about what would happen if Emmie pushed back. "What if they drop you?" they said. "Just go with it—it's only three weeks." That night, Emmie did some internet research and learned that their city had a law protecting people from gender identity discrimination. The next day,

Emmie arrived early and asked to speak with the instructor's supervisor. Emmie told the supervisor what had happened and explained that wanting to wear gender-appropriate swimwear wasn't just about personal preference but was supported by a citywide law.

The supervisor said that he'd speak with the swim instructor and that Emmie should wear their top if it made them more comfortable. After class, the instructor apologized. Emmie accepted his apology, but they weren't finished yet. They wrote to the club's management and asked if the club would adopt a nondiscrimination policy so this wouldn't happen again. Next week, Emmie walked in to find a sign explaining the new gender identity policy posted at the front desk.

Emmie was glad they hadn't given up and had figured out that *their needs were important, even if not everyone thought so at first.*

GENDER IDENTITY AT SCHOOL, AT HOME, AND IN LIFE

Coming out. It's a phrase that might make you feel hopeful, hesitant, or filled with dread. It means going public with your gender identity instead of keeping it to yourself. Why come out? The reasons are different for everyone.

Being ready to live openly as your identified gender is one of the biggest reasons you might come out. But even if you're not ready to do that, it may help to come out to a few people you trust who can help you figure out what to do next or just listen and be supportive. Having a friend or family member who knows about your identity, calls you by your chosen name and pronouns, or lets you experiment with your gender presentation around them can make a positive difference for your mental health.

You have choices in the way you come out. Some people decide to have one-on-one conversations with the people who are important to them. Others talk to their friends or family in a group all at once. For people you want to let know, but who aren't very close friends or family, a social media post might be a good way of getting the word out without having to talk to everyone in person. If you don't know where to begin, there's nothing wrong with starting the conversation with a letter. Writing a letter can help you organize your thoughts, whether or not you actually send it or give it to someone.

It's a good idea to prepare for the questions and comments people might have. If you're worried about someone's reaction, you might ask someone you trust to come along for support or meet somewhere public like a coffee shop. Even if you're pretty sure the person you're telling will be supportive, their questions could be personal or uncomfortable, or their comments might be thoughtless (even if they mean well). Make a plan to be firm about boundaries. Remember, it's not rude or mean for you to say things like:

→ "I don't want to discuss the medical stuff."

→ "Whoa, that's private!"

→ "Let's get off the subject of my body, okay?"

→ "When you say I look just like a 'real girl,' it makes it sound like you think I'm just pretending to be a girl."

→ "Please don't use the word 'shemale.' I know you're trying to be supportive, but that's actually a really hurtful and degrading term."

When you come out to someone, you might also want to talk with them about your privacy. Many people don't know that revealing someone's gender identity without their permission isn't okay. If you're not out to everyone yet, make sure the people you do come out to know who else it's okay to tell, if anyone. It's a good rule to tell only the people who have earned your trust and will be careful with your information. If someone has been careless with your secrets in the past, they have no right to know something as personal as your gender identity.

Here are a few real-life stories about coming out based on young people I've known. (To protect their privacy, all personal details have been changed.)

> **Ethan, trans boy, age 15:** "For the longest time, I felt like my friends would abandon me if they knew who I really was. I wanted to say, 'It's not me you're friends with. It's someone with a girl's name and a girl's body who isn't me.' Some of them would make stupid jokes about trans people on TV like Caitlyn Jenner, and I wanted to scream that I was one of the people they were making fun of. At first, I chose to come out only to the friends I knew would be supportive. They were so accepting that I decided to tell everyone else in an Instagram post a few weeks later. Some of the people who made trans jokes apologized. Some of them didn't. But now I don't feel like I have to be quiet anymore about this stuff."

Emily, trans girl, age 12: "I was *really* nervous because I have an older sibling who's nonbinary. I thought they were going to think I copied them! But they turned out to be really supportive and helped me come out to our parents. We sat down together, and I finally got out everything I've been wanting to say for years. My parents had a lot of questions, and I wasn't sure how to answer all of them, but in the end, they promised to support me, even if they don't understand everything about being trans. We're going to family therapy, and the therapist is helping me figure out how to transition at school. I'm so glad I don't have to stuff my clothes in the back of my closet now. I think it's brought me closer to my whole family."

Rivka, nonbinary girl, age 17: "I'm not coming out to my family anytime soon. I come from a really strict Orthodox family, and I think my parents would die if I told them who I really am—if they even know what gender identity is! The only time my family talks about gender is when they say, 'You're a man, now act like one.' Last year, they flipped out when they found out my sister in college had a lesbian roommate. I want to live as a girl someday, and I know I can reconcile my Jewish faith with my gender identity, even if my parents can't. But for now, I have to protect myself. Maybe I can just tell my sister. I wonder if she'll be able to help me when I'm ready."

Matthew, genderqueer boy, age 14: "Going public about being genderqueer was surprisingly awesome. The first time I did my nails, a lot of people at school came up to me and told me they liked them. A few people made jokes, but I had my friends around me the whole time, so it didn't bother me as much as it would if I'd been by myself. It's not always fun to be queer at my school, but it's getting better now that more and more people are coming out—even teachers. I've gotten to know people I would never have even talked to if I hadn't come out. Out of nowhere, some guy I barely know on my soccer team told me he's worried about telling his parents he's gay. It felt good to be able to help someone with something I've struggled with."

It Never Hurts to Ask for Help

Gender exploration can have some unwanted side effects. You might have to deal with bullying, or your family might not understand what you're going through. It can be hard to find support or know where to turn when things get rough. Maybe reading this workbook has already brought up some overwhelming feelings and you're not sure what to do with them.

If you're in crisis or having thoughts of suicide, contact one of these hotlines:

→ The Trans Lifeline at 1-877-565-8860 is staffed with trans peer counselors only. They are open 24/7 and guaranteed to have staff available from 10 a.m. to 4 a.m. (eastern time). The Trans Lifeline has a policy against calling the police or emergency services unless you specifically ask them to.

→ Volunteer counselors at the Trevor Project, an LGBTQ crisis line, are available 24/7. You can call 1-866-488-7386 or text START to 678-678. You can also visit TheTrevorProject.org for chat support.

→ The LGBT National Help Center can be reached at 1-888-843-4564.

→ If you're dealing with emotional or physical abuse by your family, a partner, or anyone else, contact the National Domestic Violence Hotline 24 hours a day at 1-800-799-7233. You can also chat with a counselor at TheHotline.org or text LOVEIS to 1-866-331-9474.

You might also decide to seek the help of a therapist. One way to find one is simply to Google "[name of your city/region] gender therapist." You can also visit sites like Psychology Today (PsychologyToday.com/us/therapists/transgender) to find therapists who specialize in gender identity. The World Professional Association for Transgender Health (WPATH)'s provider directory (WPATH.org /provider/search) lists therapists, primary care doctors, surgeons, and other providers who are members of that organization. Sites like TransCareSite .org and TransHealthcare.org can also help you find therapists and healthcare providers. The organization GLMA (GLMA.org) has a provider directory with healthcare providers who have identified themselves as LGBTQ friendly. (Please note the providers in these directories are not screened or guaranteed to be qualified gender specialists, though WPATH's directory allows you to search for WPATH-certified providers only.)

It can also be helpful to talk to people who are going through the same things that you are. Here are some sites that host discussions about gender identity:

→ Several **Reddit** communities host discussions on gender identity topics:

- reddit.com/r/trans
- reddit.com/r/transgender
- reddit.com/r/mtf
- reddit.com/r/ftm
- reddit.com/r/nonbinary
- reddit.com/r/asktransgender
- reddit.com/r/traaaaaaannnnnnnnnns (shortcut: reddit.com/r/traa)
- Transgender Pulse: TransgenderPulse.com/forums
- Discord servers on gender identity topics can be found in the Disboard directory at disboard.org/servers /tag/transgender

If you're looking for in-person support, your city may have an LGBTQ center that can help you with support, counseling, and sometimes healthcare or help with name changes. In general, staff at LGBTQ centers will not notify your parents or guardians that you have visited (though you should ask staff about their policies if you're concerned). You can find many of these centers at LGBTcenters.org. If there is no LGBTQ center within easy traveling distance, the nearest LGBTQ center may be able to direct you to trans groups, therapists, or other resources closer to where you live.

See the resources section (page 108) for more information.

SEXUAL ACTIVITY, CONSENT, AND STAYING SAFE

Remember when we talked about how gender is different from sexuality? Well, sexuality is different from sexual activity. You don't need to have sex to know your sexual orientation. You can use whatever label you'd like regardless of what relationships you've had in the past. In other words, experimenting with your sexuality doesn't "make" you gay, straight, or anything else.

Sometimes, it might seem like everyone's talking about sex. You might feel pressured to start before you're ready. What does "ready" mean? Your feelings are your best guide. You don't have to justify your choices about sex, even if you can't explain them. You're never obligated to do anything that makes you uncomfortable. You should also make sure not to pressure anyone else to do things that make them uncomfortable. If you decide to be sexual with a partner, check in with them frequently to make sure they're okay with what's happening.

Later, we're going to talk in more detail about sexuality. Even if you don't plan to start exploring your sexuality anytime soon, it's a good idea to read these parts of the book so you know how to stay safe when and if that time comes.

CELEBRATING THE PROCESS

Exploring your gender identity can make you feel pressured, either to make changes you might not feel right making just yet or to settle on a new identity right away. People might have questions like: *Have you decided on a new name? Is this permanent? Are you going to transition? When are you going to be "done" transitioning?*

It's easy to get caught up in wanting to get to the "end" and forget that the process of gender exploration or gender transition can be exciting and enlightening in itself. If you've watched shows about trans people, you may have noticed that many of them portray transition as a huge, dramatic struggle with a lot of tears and heartbreak. This *might* be true of yours, too, but it doesn't have to be.

Your gender journey can be one, some, or all of these things:

→ **Fun:** trying on new outfits, getting to know your sense of style

→ **Affirming:** finding out that other people are willing to accept you as you are

→ **Validating:** finding out that your feelings reflect something real and important about yourself

→ **Educational:** learning about trans pioneers in history

→ **Creative:** writing and making art about your gender journey

- → **Sensual:** figuring out what you like about your body, exploring your sexuality

- → **Friendly:** seeking out other gender variant and queer people in your community

- → **Adventurous:** doing things you were scared to do before you felt at home in your body or identity

- → **Spiritual:** finding gender variant people in your religion's texts and history, figuring out how your beliefs mesh with your gender identity

The bottom line is this: don't forget to have a good trip, even if you're impatient to get to your destination.

Gender Identity Trailblazer: Lou Sullivan (1951–1991)

Louis Graydon Sullivan was an author and activist who fought for recognition of trans men at a time when it was hard for trans men to get transition-related treatment if they didn't conform to stereotypes. Sullivan, an out gay man, was rejected by gender clinics because of his sexual orientation. But he refused to hide his gay identity, instead working to end clinics' restrictions on gay trans men who wanted to physically transition.

Sullivan kept diaries, writing about his experiences in a passionate, poetic, and sometimes fragmented way. At age 15, he wrote, "I want to look like what I am but don't know what someone like me looks like." He began living as a man in the 1970s. Eventually, Sullivan was able to get testosterone therapy, which (in his words) made him feel "sensual + strong + vibrant," and later he was able to receive gender confirmation surgeries.

In 1991, Sullivan died of complications from AIDS. In 2019, Sullivan's name was included in New York's National LGBTQ Wall of Honor, and he was inducted into San Francisco's Rainbow Honor Walk. His diaries were published in abridged form as *We Both Laughed in Pleasure*.

BE HONEST AND HONOR YOUR FEELINGS

This workbook is going to ask you to dig deep. Some of the feelings that come up might not be ones that you've let yourself feel before. You're going to be asked to question assumptions you might be making about yourself and the world around you. This can be a little scary, but it's going to pay off.

What you get out of it is going to depend on your willingness to be honest with yourself. In particular, you're going to be asked to treat your own feelings with the respect they deserve. If you're used to being treated like you don't know what you're talking about, this might feel weird, and you might need some practice letting yourself believe . . . well, yourself.

Let's do one final exercise before we dive into part 2. Write a few sentences about how you're feeling about your gender identity right at this moment—positive thoughts, negative thoughts, or a mix. Return to this part of the workbook after you've finished it to reflect on how your understanding of yourself has changed and grown.

_____

_____

_____

_____

_____

That wraps up the first leg of our trip. You've come so far! You've learned about the different aspects of gender identity and expression, expanded your vocabulary, and done some serious reflection about your life, identity, and feelings. You're ready to move on to the next part, where we're going to progress through a series of exercises that will help you gain a fuller understanding of your gender and figure out what you want to do next.

PART 2

EXERCISES TO EXPLORE YOUR IDENTITY, UNDERSTAND YOURSELF, AND EXPRESS THE AUTHENTIC YOU

These interactive exercises are going to help you think deeply about your gender identity, deal with powerful emotions, and learn how to assert yourself with other people. We'll talk about some tough topics, like being your authentic self, communicating with people about your gender identity, dealing with bullies, and keeping yourself safe.

LET YOUR MIND WANDER

As you work through the exercises, it's important to be open to the feelings that come to you. Make sure you're not telling yourself not to feel what you feel. You can say, "That's not possible for me *right now*" or "I don't want to think about that *at this moment*," but don't cut yourself off from experiences that you might want to have in the future or feelings that seem confusing right now. You can always revisit these feelings, wants, and needs later when you have more perspective.

EXERCISE: WHAT IF?

Gender exploration or transition can make you happier, but it can also make new anxieties pop up, like not being accepted by other people or meeting people who are rude or ignorant.

Some people are prone to **catastrophic thinking**, which means imagining the worst thing that could happen. When things get intense, they may convince themselves that the worst outcome *will* come true, no matter how unlikely it is. This thinking may prevent them from making *any* changes in their life because they're convinced that terrible things are going to happen if they do.

Here are some examples of catastrophic thinking:

→ "If I transition, no one is ever going to want to date me, and I'll be alone forever."

→ "If I come out as trans to my church, they'll kick me out."

→ "If someone makes fun of how I look, I'll have a nervous breakdown and have to switch schools."

→ "If I tell my brother I'm nonbinary, he'll never speak to me again."

→ "If I wear makeup to school, everyone is going to think I'm weird, and I'm not going to have any friends this year."

One way to deal with this type of anxiety is **decatastrophizing**, which is a way of thinking about scary situations that allows you to push past your fears. Instead of obsessing about how awful it would be if something bad happened, you think about how realistic the scary situation is, how bad it would *really* be, and how you could cope if it did happen.

Let's practice this technique. Here's an example to show how it works . . .

WHAT IF . . . I TOLD MY EXTENDED FAMILY ABOUT MY NEW NAME AND PRONOUNS?

What is the worst thing that could happen?

My relatives could refuse to use my new name and pronouns. They could tell me I'm not really trans or that it's a phase.

What would be bad about that?

I would feel really upset if they called me by the wrong name and pronouns. Birthdays and holidays would be awkward, and I wouldn't feel welcome.

How likely is it that this will *really* happen?

VERY UNLIKELY ←———————X———————→ 100% CERTAIN

What is the evidence that it will happen? What is the evidence that it won't?

My grandma is old, and I don't know if she knows what being trans is. My cousins are kind of conservative, but I haven't heard them say anything bad about LGBTQ+ people. My mom's side of the family has a couple of gay relatives, and everyone seems to support them.

If it *did* happen, how would I deal with it?

I would speak up. I could also ask my siblings and other supportive family members to speak up. If they kept misgendering me or said anything mean, I would leave.

If it *did* happen, would I be okay six months from now?

- ☐ Yes
- ☑ Probably
- ☐ Probably not
- ☐ No

Now it's your turn. Pick something about gender exploration or transition that makes you anxious.

What if . . .

_____

_____

What is the worst thing that could happen?

_____

_____

What would be bad about that?

_____

_____

How likely is it that this will *really* happen?

VERY UNLIKELY   **100% CERTAIN**

←—————————————————————————————→

What is the evidence that it will happen? What is the evidence that it won't?

_____

_____

_____

If it *did* happen, how would I deal with it?

_____

_____

_____

If it *did* happen, would I be okay six months from now?

☐ Yes

☐ Probably not

☐ Probably

☐ No

Try the exercise again, picking something else about gender exploration or transition that makes you anxious.

What if . . .

_____

_____

_____

_____

_____

What is the worst thing that could happen?

_____

_____

_____

_____

_____

What would be bad about that?

_____

_____

_____

_____

_____

How likely is it that this will *really* happen?

VERY UNLIKELY   100% CERTAIN

← ——→

What is the evidence that it will happen? What is the evidence that it won't?

_____

_____

_____

_____

_____

If it *did* happen, how would I deal with it?

_____

_____

_____

_____

If it *did* happen, would I be okay six months from now?

☐ Yes   ☐ Probably not

☐ Probably   ☐ No

Before, you might not have thoroughly thought about how likely bad outcomes were to happen. Now, you might find they're not as likely to happen as you thought. And you may not have considered how your coping skills could help you even if the worst *did* happen.

Over the next few years, you're going to learn that you can handle "catastrophic situations" better than you think.

EXERCISE: SONG OF MYSELF

Have you ever run into your teacher while out with your friends? Did you straighten up a little or change how you were talking? When we're with different people, we *are* different people. We might even give up who we are in some ways to get along with others.

Gender expression can be like this. You may feel safe expressing your gender fully around some people, while with others, you may censor yourself. Maybe your safety depends on it, or maybe you just don't want to have to answer weird questions. It can be hard to balance being cautious and hiding so much of yourself that you don't feel like you can ever relax.

For this exercise, write in the left column about the version of yourself that comes out when you're alone or with people you trust. In the right column, write about the way you act around people you don't know very well.

	PRIVATE SELF	PUBLIC SELF
The way I walk and talk		
The things I enjoy doing		
My clothes and hair		
My romantic attractions		
My hopes for the future		

If there's a big difference between your private self and public self, you might want to think about letting more of your inner self into your outer life. See "On Your Fantasy Island" (page 41) for ways to dive into your innermost hopes and dreams or "A Safe Way Forward" (page 51) for practical steps for getting your inner self out there.

EXERCISE: PRONOUNS ARE LIKE HATS

The great thing about pronouns is that you can try them on and see what fits without having to commit.

Practice saying the following sentences using he/him/his, she/her/hers, they/them/their(s), ze/zir/zirs, or another pronoun set of your choice. Try all of them and see what feels right to you.

→ Yellow is _____ favorite color.

_____ like(s) that color more than blue.

→ _____ is/are taking geometry next semester.

→ I don't know _____ phone number. Ask _____.

→ _____ desk is over there. The stapler on top is _____.

→ Does/do _____ want to go for lunch?

→ I told _____ to be here half an hour ago. Call _____ and see if

_____

's/'re on _____ way.

EXERCISE: CONFRONTING YOUR DEMONS

What are your demons—those horrible little creatures that keep you from feeling good about yourself or doing things you enjoy? Maybe you have demons named "anxiety," "bullies," or "bathroom fears." Name your demons. Give them personalities. But most importantly, give them a weakness!

Demon #1's name is _____.

Their personality is _____.

This demon keeps me from _____ and makes me feel _____.

This demon's weakness is _____.

When I say the words _____ and think of something comforting like _____, this demon is banished.

Demon #2's name is _____.

Their personality is _____.

This demon keeps me from _____ and makes me feel _____.

This demon's weakness is _____.

When I say the words _____ and think of something comforting like _____, this demon is banished.

EXERCISE: FEELING A LITTLE OUT OF PLACE

In part 1, we talked about gender dysphoria: uncomfortable feelings about how your body looks or feels or the way other people see you. It can sometimes be hard to figure out whether dysphoria is actually what you're feeling. Maybe you know that your identified gender and your gender assigned at birth aren't in sync, but you don't feel dysphoria is an accurate description.

If you're sure dysphoria isn't a factor in your life, you can skip this exercise. Otherwise, check off each of the following statements you agree with.

☐ When I speak, my voice sounds like the wrong gender, and it makes me uncomfortable.

☐ I sometimes have happy fantasies about being a gender other than my assigned gender.

☐ In the past, I've found excuses to pretend to be a gender other than my assigned gender for Halloween or as an actor in a play.

☐ Being seen as another gender makes me feel happier and more comfortable.

☐ I want other people to see me as a different gender than the one assigned to me at birth.

☐ Hiding certain parts of my body makes me feel better.

☐ If I could wave a wand and change the gender features of my body, I'd do it right now.

☐ When I dream about my future life, I think of myself as a different gender than I am now.

☐ If everyone could suddenly see me as another gender, I'd be so happy.

☐ Thoughts I've been having about changing my gender features are taking up a lot of my time.

☐ I want my chest, genitals, body hair, or other body parts to change.

☐ I wish I could wake up tomorrow and look exactly like the gender I am inside—even if I don't know 100 percent what that would look like.

☐ I know I'd be happier if I took steps to live as another gender.

Did you check any statements? How many do you think you need for your dysphoria to be "real"? If you checked even one statement, it's likely that what you're feeling is some degree of gender dysphoria. This may be something to discuss with a therapist.

Regardless of how many statements you checked, your inner feelings about your gender are the only permission you need to make the changes you'd like to make or adopt a gender label that fits you. Though it would be helpful, nobody gets a single clear sign that says, "You are definitely gender variant—really, truly, 100 percent."

If you didn't check any of the statements, you might not be experiencing gender dysphoria. Maybe what needs to change is your gender *expression*—for example, your clothes or your hair—not your body or identity labels. (If that's the case, the next exercise will be right up your alley.) Or maybe you've found that you're happy with yourself the way you are now. That's great! Maybe you just needed reassurance that the way you feel and express yourself is okay.

EXERCISE: FITS LIKE A GLOVE

What are some types and styles of clothing and accessories you *never* wear? Write them down.

Pants/skirts:	Tops/shirts:
Dresses/jumpsuits:	Hats/hair accessories:
Shoes/socks:	Jewelry and accessories:
Makeup/nail polish:	Patterns and fabrics:

Did you describe stuff that you find hideous, boring, or not expressive of who you are? Or did you describe clothing and accessories that just feel a little scary? Maybe they're items you'd like to wear, but you don't feel comfortable wearing them because of your assigned gender, body type, or current style. Take some time to reflect on *why* you never wear these things.

EXERCISE: GENDER EUPHORIA

As mentioned before, gender dysphoria is the feeling that something's wrong about your body or the way other people see you. Gender *euphoria* is the opposite—the feeling that comes from things being *right*. You might feel euphoria when people gender you correctly, when you see the new muscles you've developed from working out, or when your makeup looks just right. Let's do an exercise to explore gender euphoria.

What gives you the most gender euphoria about your *appearance*? (Examples might include "wearing my favorite shirt" or "having a pretty face.")

_____

_____

What about your *interactions with other people* makes you feel gender euphoria? (Examples might include "being referred to as 'he' in music class" or "being called cute.")

_____

_____

What *imaginary situations* give you gender euphoria? (Examples might include "thinking about having a flat chest" or "visualizing myself at the beach wearing a bikini.")

_____

_____

Put this exercise aside for five or ten minutes and then take a look at what you wrote. Would you say you relate more to the positive aspects of gender variance than the negative ones? For example, do you not care much when someone calls you "she" but feel very happy when someone calls you "he"?

If so, then gender euphoria might be a better way of describing your feelings than gender dysphoria. When you're thinking about changes you might want to make in the future, it might be more helpful to think about what you're moving *toward* rather than what you're moving *away* from.

EXERCISE: SELF-CARE ISN'T JUST BUBBLE BATHS

What's self-care all about? Self-care is really about priorities. Caring for yourself means prioritizing things that are important to you and giving less importance to things that can wait.

Self-care can include more obvious things like relaxation or body care, but it's also about making time for other things that matter. Maybe you do a lot for other people and need to put yourself first. Maybe you have gender identity concerns that you're just now realizing are important and worthy of your time.

Use the "priority organizer" to get your priorities straight. Sort the stuff in your life into high, medium, and low priority by writing them in the following boxes.

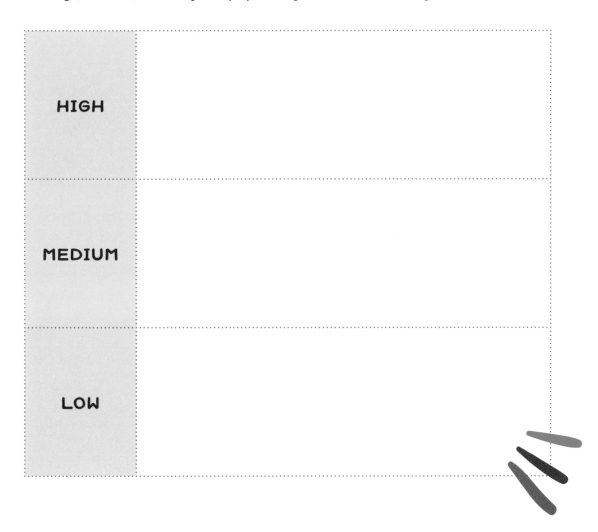

HIGH	
MEDIUM	
LOW	

EXERCISE: LAYING THE FOUNDATION

Sometimes, the future feels so uncertain that it seems weird to make plans. Who knows where you're going to be in five, ten, or twenty years? How can you possibly know where your gender exploration is going to take you?

Even if your goals are far in the future, you can still do small things today that will help you achieve them. This could mean studying hard so you can go to a college with a LGBTQ-friendly campus or saving money for a new wardrobe.

To get to where you want to be **next month**, what do you have to do **this week**?

_____

_____

_____

_____

To get to where you want to be **next year**, what do you have to do **this month**?

_____

_____

_____

_____

To get to where you want to be **five years from now**, what do you have to do **this year**?

_____

_____

_____

_____

EXERCISE: ON YOUR FANTASY ISLAND

If you lived in a perfect world, what would you look like? How would you dress? How would you present yourself to the world? Chances are, that person you're imagining is at least a little different from who you are right now. The fantasies you have in private—in your brain, where no one else can see, or at home in your room with the door locked—say something important about your gender identity.

Let's do some creative writing. Imagine an island where everyone accepts you as you are. If that's too public, picture an island where you're totally alone. In a perfect world, where there's no one to say "that's ridiculous" or "that doesn't fit you," who would you be?

On your fantasy island, how would people see you? Think about the most important characteristics you'd want people to notice when they look at you.

_____

_____

_____

_____

_____

On your fantasy island, what would your body look like?

_____

_____

_____

_____

_____

On your fantasy island, what would you wear? What clothes and makeup (if any) would you use to make your body look its best? Don't be concerned about whether these clothes would actually look good on you in real life.

_____

_____

_____

_____

_____

On your fantasy island, what would your social self be like? Would you have masculine mannerisms or feminine ones? Maybe both, or neither? How would you relate to other people? Would your behavior change from day to day?

_____

_____

_____

_____

_____

On your fantasy island, who would be around you? Whom would you date? What kinds of people would you be friends with?

_____

_____

_____

_____

_____

On your fantasy island, where would you live? What would your house look like? Your bedroom? Your town?

_____

_____

_____

_____

_____

Maybe the "fantasy island you" isn't like you in real life at all. Maybe some parts of your fantasy life aren't even possible for you or for anyone. But there are surely things about your fantasy life that you connect with on a deep level because they reflect authentic feelings about who you are, how you'd like to look, and what kind of future life you'd like to have.

Pay attention to those feelings. Even if some of these desires and wishes seem far off, some of them may be worth working toward. For instance, your fantasy may reflect a wish to become more independent, pursue your passions, or find people who click with you.

Come back to this exercise in the future if you're thinking about making changes in your life and want to take a deep dive into your dreams.

EXERCISE: WORKING ON YOURSELF

Your physical body affects how you see yourself and how others see you and is powerfully connected to your gender identity. But when you experience dysphoria or feel disconnected from your body, it's easy to neglect yourself.

On the arrows, mark an X where your habits fall.

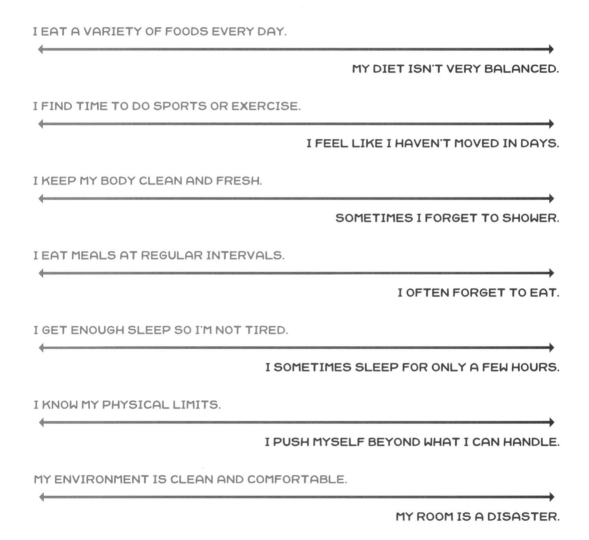

I EAT A VARIETY OF FOODS EVERY DAY.

MY DIET ISN'T VERY BALANCED.

I FIND TIME TO DO SPORTS OR EXERCISE.

I FEEL LIKE I HAVEN'T MOVED IN DAYS.

I KEEP MY BODY CLEAN AND FRESH.

SOMETIMES I FORGET TO SHOWER.

I EAT MEALS AT REGULAR INTERVALS.

I OFTEN FORGET TO EAT.

I GET ENOUGH SLEEP SO I'M NOT TIRED.

I SOMETIMES SLEEP FOR ONLY A FEW HOURS.

I KNOW MY PHYSICAL LIMITS.

I PUSH MYSELF BEYOND WHAT I CAN HANDLE.

MY ENVIRONMENT IS CLEAN AND COMFORTABLE.

MY ROOM IS A DISASTER.

If your marks are more on the right side of the arrows, turn to "Self-Care Isn't Just Bubble Baths" (page 39) for an exercise about how to put caring for yourself first. If you're really feeling unable to care for yourself no matter how much time you have, that's a sign that it's time to see a therapist or talk to someone you trust about your mental health.

EXERCISE: PACK UP YOUR TROUBLES

We all have them: those embarrassing memories that keep coming back to us just as we're about to drift off to sleep. In the course of your gender exploration, you might have said, done, or worn something you cringe about now. Perhaps you had a hair-gel disaster or took a spill in some heels in front of everyone. Maybe these memories are holding you back from trying new things or asserting yourself.

Write down each of your embarrassing moments on a separate piece of paper. Fold them up as tightly as you can, like you're packing clothes. Put them in the smallest box you can find (your troubles' mini-suitcase) and stick it in the back of your closet. Write a date on your calendar three months from now and take the box out then. See if you're still bothered by your embarrassing moments. Chances are, at least some of the embarrassment will have faded, and you might even wonder why they embarrassed you at all.

EXERCISE: DOUBLE-SHOT HALF-CAF EXTRA-SPRINKLES YOU

Have you found that some of these exercises speak to you more than others? For example, clothes might be a really important part of your identity, while your physical body isn't. Or you might feel like what's in your brain is the only thing that matters, and the outside stuff doesn't matter much at all.

Use this exercise to dig deeper into what's important to you. Fill in the "latte" of your gender identity.

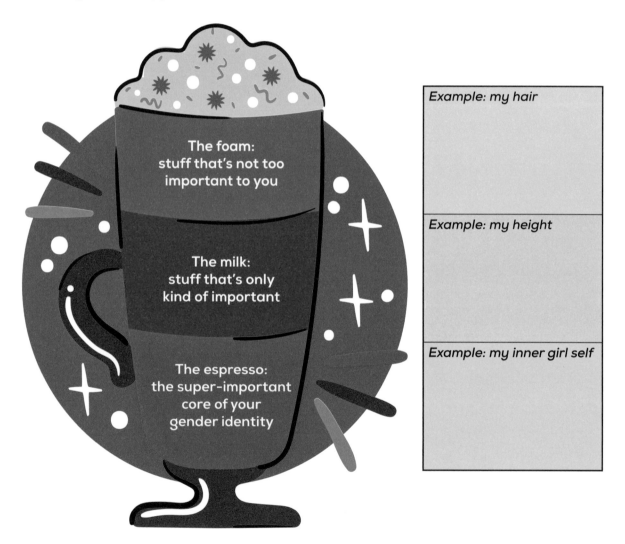

The foam: stuff that's not too important to you

The milk: stuff that's only kind of important

The espresso: the super-important core of your gender identity

Example: my hair

Example: my height

Example: my inner girl self

EXERCISE: A CONFIDENCE GAME

"You just have to have confidence." How many times have you heard that? I'm not going to tell you to have confidence, but I *am* going to tell you that you've probably had confidence in the past without knowing it. By channeling that confidence, you can get through pretty much any situation.

For this exercise, you're going to write about times you've been brave and faced difficult tasks.

First, write about a time when you faced a **social situation** that made you nervous.

_____

_____

_____

What skills or techniques helped you get through it?

_____

_____

_____

Was there a time when you faced a challenging **academic task**, like a hard test?

_____

_____

_____

What did you do to keep yourself calm and power through it?

_____

_____

_____

EXERCISE: DEAR KID ME

You may not feel like you have things all figured out now, but guess who had things even *less* figured out? Younger you.

What kinds of things would you like to share with your elementary-school self? What have you figured out about your gender identity that would clear up a lot of confusion for that little person? Write a letter to your kid self.

_____

_____

_____

_____

_____

_____

_____

_____

_____

_____

_____

_____

_____

_____

EXERCISE: CARRYING THAT WEIGHT

Many gender variant people carry a lot of tension in their bodies. Sometimes, it's the result of stress. It can also come from physical habits, like hunching over or hiding certain body parts. You might not notice this tension until you feel a pain in your neck or a twinge in your back.

Lie on your back in a comfortable place and close your eyes. Mentally scan your body, focusing on the top of your head first and moving downward. When you're finished, notice where you feel tension. Check the area(s) here.

☐ Head   ☐ Lower back

☐ Shoulders   ☐ Feet

☐ Upper back   ☐ Neck

☐ Calves   ☐ Hands

☐ Face   ☐ Thighs

☐ Arms

Think about setting aside some time every day to work out that tension with simple stretching, yoga, or self-massage. You can also use a technique called **progressive relaxation**: tense up all of your muscles at once, then slowly relax them one by one, starting at your head and working your way down.

After trying to release some tension, do you feel any different? Reflect on that here.

_____

_____

_____

_____

_____

_____

EXERCISE: AM I REAL?

What makes a "real man"? What should a "real woman" look like? It's possible you've been wondering if you're "real." In the following space, write three or four sentences about what you think makes someone "really" the gender they are.

_____

_____

_____

_____

_____

_____

_____

_____

Read what you just wrote. Are your ideas based on a person's inner identity or on stereotypes? Do your ideas make your own gender identity seem less valid?

Some people say that to be "really" trans or nonbinary, you had to know you were gender variant when you were a toddler, or have gender-affirming surgery, or some other made-up rule. None of these are true. You're the only person who can say what your identity is.

EXERCISE: A SAFE WAY FORWARD

Let's talk about coming out. You might think coming out is an all-at-once process, but when you're transitioning or expressing your gender more fully, it's likely the process will happen in steps.

Think about all the people in your life: close friends, parents, distant cousins, grandparents, stepsiblings, and that weird guy in math class. If you decide to come out and live your identity more openly, which of these people need to know about it?

Let's start with the most important people. Who is so close to you that you would definitely want them to know about your gender identity?

_____

_____

_____

Who needs to know about your gender identity because of practical reasons? (For example, your teachers, so they call you by the right name.)

_____

_____

_____

Who *doesn't* need to know about your gender identity? Perhaps they're not a safe person for you right now, or they're not close enough to you for it to matter. (For example, an aunt you haven't seen in years.)

_____

_____

_____

Come back to this exercise when you're ready to tell more people about your gender identity. Keep in mind that there are no "shoulds." You don't have to come out to someone just because you're related or because they ask you about your gender. Whom you tell and when you tell them is entirely up to you.

EXERCISE: IT'S ME ON TV!

If you love making art or writing stories, this exercise is for you. Your job: create a gender variant character better than the ones you've found in books, on TV, or in movies. Representation in the media matters! But why?

Stereotypes (overly simplistic ideas about a type of person) and misrepresentation can affect how you think about yourself and spread harmful myths to the people around you. You might know immediately when a gender variant character is badly written. But it's important to be able to figure out *why* you feel that way.

What stereotypes have you seen in TV shows and movies about gender variant people? What have you heard from others who have seen stereotypes or misrepresented gender variant people in media? On the flip side, what *positive* representations have you found? Have you ever seen a queer or gender variant character whose experiences spoke to you? Has a book or film ever changed your life?

Use these questions to spark your creativity. Maybe you'll end up creating a character who changes someone else's life!

What's your character's name?

_____

_____

_____

What are their pronouns?

_____

_____

_____

What's their backstory (the story of their life to this point)?

_____

_____

_____

_____

_____

What kind of world do they live in?

_____

_____

_____

_____

_____

What's their mission or goal?

_____

_____

_____

How are they different from other gender variant characters?

_____

_____

_____

What do you think people could learn from your character?

_____

_____

_____

What does your character look like? Draw them in this box.

EXERCISE: A SERIES OF TUBES

Queer communities on the internet can offer you support and advice. They can also make you feel like crap. Not everyone in the LGBTQ community is nice. Some people think that gender variant people don't belong in the same group as gays, lesbians, and bisexuals. Other people feel that they have the right to decide that your gender identity isn't valid. Though some people are friendly, you might feel bad if you're constantly comparing your life and experiences to theirs.

Check the statements that sound like online experiences you've had.

☐ My dysphoria has gotten worse because the people I've seen online look so much better than I do. I feel like I'll never get there.

☐ I got a lot of supportive comments on that selfie I posted, but I also got a lot of weird, sexual, and downright mean ones.

☐ I get scared when I read people's posts about bad experiences after coming out.

☐ I have to physically stop myself from reading comments on news articles about trans issues because of all the trolls.

☐ I was pretty confident about my gender identity before I saw people on the internet criticizing people with the same identity and telling them they weren't valid.

☐ It's hard to find sites that don't have toxic people taking over threads and yelling at everyone else.

☐ Some of the discussions I've had online about trans issues have been so negative. I'm not sad about my life. Why is everyone else?

If you checked more than one of these statements, it might be time to step back and think about how you interact with people online. Remember, you have the choice to seek out people who support your identity—and you. Online, jerks are much louder than other people, and they often drive away nicer people from communities. Try to find communities with strong discussion rules, good moderation, and a healthy culture.

EXERCISE: FINDING YOUR DIGITAL SPACE

Connecting with other gender variant people online is a great way to get support and help with what you're going through, especially when it isn't safe to talk to your family and friends. But online safety and security are important, too. You might be wondering if someone online who's not so nice could find you in real life, break into your accounts, or post your personal information publicly. If you're not out in real life, it might be hard to get support if someone is harassing you online.

Let's do a checkup of your online activity. Circle your answer to each question in the following quiz. Then, give yourself 1 point for every *a* answer, 2 points for every *b*, and 3 points for every *c*.

1. When you post online in a place where anyone can read your posts, what kind of avatar do you use?
   a. A photo of my full face.
   b. A partial face photo or a realistic drawing of me.
   c. A photo or drawing that isn't me or a cartoon/nonrealistic drawing of me.

2. What kinds of details have you given out online in the past?
   a. Lots of things: name, gender, hometown, name of school, hobbies.
   b. A few minor details, like my state and my first name.
   c. Nothing. I make sure to censor anything that could identify me.

3. Have you ever sent an online friend information that you wouldn't post publicly?
   a. Sure. I have friends I've never met in real life that I trust enough to know all my personal details.
   b. Only when I'm pretty sure the other person really is who they say they are.
   c. Never. If I don't know the person and trust them in real life, they don't get my info.

4. Have you ever accidentally given out more information than you intended?
   a. That happens a lot. I've had to delete stuff after realizing I put out more info about myself than I planned to.
   b. That's happened one or two times. Sometimes, I don't realize how much personal info is in my posts.
   c. That hasn't happened yet. I look through my posts carefully before I hit "send."

5. Would you ever meet someone in real life after exchanging messages online?

    a. Sure. If I feel like I know them well enough, I'd meet them, even if I'd never seen them before.

    b. I'd do it only if I was pretty sure I knew who they were.

    c. I wouldn't. Or I'd do it only if we met in a public place and one of my parents or guardians was there with me.

6. Your passwords are . . .

    a. The same for every site.

    b. A few different versions of the same thing.

    c. Different for every site I use regularly.

YOUR SCORE: _____

If you scored 6-11: You might want to take a serious look at what you're putting out on the internet. Even if you haven't encountered anyone who wants to invade your privacy or harm you, it could happen unexpectedly, and you might find it hard to keep your private information from spreading once it's out there. Turn to page 84 in part 3 to learn more about privacy and security online.

If you scored 11-15: You're taking steps to protect your privacy, but you might want to check your posts more carefully for identifying information and be more careful about what you send to other people. Remember, private messages can be shared, and small details can be used to identify you.

If you scored 15+: Great work! You've done a good job keeping your information safe. Share your skills with your friends if you think they're making themselves vulnerable to predators or scammers.

EXERCISE: DON'T FENCE ME IN

You probably already know it's tough to express yourself when other people have strict expectations about how you should dress, look, and act. If you're exploring your gender or transitioning right now, you might feel pressured to be like certain stereotypes or be super-masculine or super-feminine, even if it's not your style.

If you're a trans guy, maybe you don't feel like you can wear a pink sweater in public because you're afraid people won't take you seriously as a male. Or maybe you're non-binary and feel like you have to wear androgynous clothes all the time, even if you *really* want to put on the fancy dress in the back of your closet. Maybe you're getting pushback from others no matter what you do.

This exercise will help you work through these feelings. In the left column, write something you'd like to do, wear, or express in the future. In the right column, write about a stereotype that's stopping you from doing that.

I WANT TO . . .	BUT I DON'T WANT PEOPLE TO THINK I'M . . .
Join the weight-lifting club	Masculine
Date guys	A girl

Maybe you're not comfortable doing the things you wrote about right now. But it's possible these feelings will change once you feel more comfortable in your own skin. You might also get better at pushing back against other people's expectations.

Come back to this exercise in a few weeks, months, or even years to see how far you've progressed.

THINGS I'VE TRIED . . .	HOW I FEEL NOW . . .

EXERCISE: THE DOCTOR IS IN

No matter what your gender is, getting medical care can be an uncomfortable experience. Your doctor may have to examine parts of your body that make you feel embarrassed. You also might still be seeing the same doctor you had when you were a child, and they might call you by your old name or pronouns even if you go by new ones now. Maybe you're feeling like you don't have a lot of control over your medical care.

This exercise is about the ways you can make yourself feel more comfortable during a medical visit, prepare for what's going to happen, and assert yourself to the people providing your care.

Write your answers to the following questions.

What might you need to do to assert yourself during this visit? (For example, "I may need to remind the receptionist that my name is Isabelle now, not Eric" or "I need to tell the doctor that I want to see her by myself without my parents in the room.")

_____

_____

_____

_____

What can you do to practice being assertive before this visit? (For example, "I can role-play with my mom how I'll tell the doctor that I'm using they/them pronouns now" or "I can practice asking the questions I need to ask in the mirror.")

_____

_____

_____

_____

What questions do you need to ask during this visit? (For example, "I want to know if the doctor can keep what I say during this visit confidential" or "I need to ask if the side effects of my acne medication are normal.")

_____

_____

_____

_____

_____

What can you do to make yourself less nervous during the visit? If you know the visit is going to make you nervous or uncomfortable no matter what you do, what can you do to calm down afterward? (For example, "After my appointment, I'm going to make myself a mug cake" or "I'm going to listen to my favorite podcast for an hour.")

_____

_____

_____

_____

_____

Making Yourself Heard

Here are a few tips to help you get the healthcare you deserve:

→ It's okay to let your healthcare providers know if you're nervous about medical exams and procedures. You can always ask what's going to happen and why. You can say, "Can you tell me what you're going to do before you do it?" so you're not surprised.

→ You can ask to see your healthcare provider alone if you're embarrassed to have your parents or guardians in the exam room or if you have private questions. A good healthcare provider will honor this request. If there's something others need to know, your provider can bring them in after the exam.

→ Even if you haven't medically transitioned, it's still a good idea to try to find trans- or gender variant–friendly healthcare providers. Clinics that serve a lot of gender variant patients are more likely to respect your pronouns and be more mindful of your feelings around your body. Check out page 18 for tips on finding providers that serve trans and gender variant patients.

EXERCISE: UNCERTAIN TIMES

Right now, you might be deciding whether to come out to people about your gender identity. Or you might find yourself asking, "How do I know who I really am? What if I'm not who I think I am?" Saying your identity out loud can be scary, even if there aren't any serious consequences.

This quiz will help you become more aware of how you deal with the unknowns, uncertainties, and what-ifs of life. Circle your response to each question.

1. Which is truer about you?
   a. I need to know exactly what the future holds before I make decisions, whether it's the college I choose, the people I date, or the things I buy.

   b. I know I can't predict the future, so I don't stress about unknowns.

2. What would happen if you decided to explore an identity and then found out that it wasn't a good fit?
   a. I'd be lost. Everything I knew about myself would be in doubt.

   b. I could handle it. Sometimes you have to experiment a little to know who you are.

3. How would you feel if you knew you'd never be 100 percent sure of your gender identity?
   a. Awful. If I'm not 100 percent sure about something, I can't move forward.

   b. Okay. It's tough to be 100 percent sure of anything, but especially something complicated like gender identity.

4. True or false: Even if a doubt is very small, it might still stop me from making a decision about something important.
   a. True. Little things I'm not sure about keep me awake at night.

   b. False. I think about the pros and cons of my decisions, but I don't obsess over tiny doubts.

5. Would you ever say, "I don't have to know exactly what my gender identity is right now; I can wait for the answer to come to me, even if it takes a while"?
   a. No! I want to know now. I hate being unsure!

   b. Yes. I'm comfortable taking the time needed to figure things out.

6. True or false: The risk of making the wrong choice always matters more than the benefit of making the right choice.
   a. True. Regret is my number-one fear when I make any decision!
   b. False. Sometimes, you have to take a risk for something that makes you happy.

7. "If I told someone my gender identity was X and it later turned out to be Y, I'd feel . . ."
   a. Devastated. No one would ever believe me about my identity again.
   b. Fine. There's no shame in finding a better way to describe how I feel.

If you picked **more a than b answers**: Predictability, control, and certainty are important to you. You're afraid of doing the wrong thing, so it's sometimes hard for you to do anything at all, even if it's something you really want to do. Being careful can be a good thing, but it can also backfire if it stops you from making decisions completely. You might want to carefully introduce more risk and uncertainty into your life. It's hard to go through life without taking *any* risks!

If you picked **more b than a answers**: You like flexibility more than predictability. You're okay with not knowing everything about your future. You might make the wrong decisions sometimes, but you know you can change course when that happens. You're confident making a leap when there are good things on the other side. It sounds like you're ready to deal with the uncertainties that come with exploring your gender.

EXERCISE: YOU OUGHTA KNOW

Chances are, there are a few things you know about yourself and your gender by now that other people don't know. Here's a chance to reflect on what those things are and which ones you'd like to share with the world.

Let's do some journaling. Set a timer for five minutes and spend that time writing about the things you want people to know about you and your gender. You can write about what you'd like people to know in the future when you're ready to share your gender identity with the world or what you want everyone to know right now. Don't change what you've written or go back and correct anything. Just keep going until the timer goes off.

Here are some prompts to get you started:

→ If I could instantly make everyone understand one thing about me, it would be . . .

→ Sometimes I worry that people don't know . . .

→ I want people to look at me and say . . .

→ My family gets _____ wrong about me.

→ I like _____ about myself, and I want other people to like it, too.

→ Friends who understand me well know that . . .

_____

_____

_____

_____

_____

_____

_____

EXERCISE: A WORD WITH YOURSELF

The words you use to describe yourself can communicate a lot of information about your identity—not just to other people but to yourself. So can the words other people use to describe you. Maybe you cringe when your parents call you "our little princess." Or maybe you call yourself "glittery" when everyone else calls you "the Hulk."

In the following table, write words that you think describe you really well in the left column. In the middle column, write words that you're not sure describe you, only partly describe you, or describe you only at certain times. In the right column, write words that don't describe you at all.

Here are some words to get you started. Feel free to add your own. Don't spend too much time on any one word.

man	handsome	mysterious	glam
woman	femme	genderless	sparkly
boy	butch	Amazonian	rugged
girl	androgynous	graceful	mermaid
diva	goddess	in-between	lumberjack
prince	boi	foxy	delicate
princess	shape-shifter	stalwart	aggressive
soft	witch	fairy	swashbuckling

YES!	MEH . . .	NO WAY!

Take a look at the columns. Notice any themes? Are the words in the left column more masculine or more feminine? Both? Neither? Did you say "no way" to specific types of words? These are all valuable clues about what might be lurking in that sparkly, fierce, or swashbuckling brain of yours.

EXERCISE: COMMUNITY TIES

This quiz is about getting out into the real world of queer and gender variant people. Finding queer friends can be awesome! "Finally," you say, "I get to meet people like me." But maybe you're wondering if you'll fit in with them, or maybe you're not sure you want to meet them at all.

Let's dive in. Circle the answer that best finishes each statement.

1. If I joined an LGBTQ group . . .

   a. I'm sure I'd fit right in. (Or: I already do fit in.)

   b. I'd want to fit in, but I don't know if I would.

   c. I don't think I'd have anything in common with them.

2. I look at the gender variant people at my school or in my community and think . . .

   a. I'm a lot like those people. They're part of my community.

   b. I would like to be part of their community, but maybe they wouldn't accept me.

   c. Those people aren't me at all. We don't have much in common.

3. Groups and activities for queer people in my area seem . . .

   a. Welcoming. I think I'd like to join them sometime, or I already do.

   b. A little scary. What if they reject me?

   c. *Very* scary. I don't know what would happen if I joined them, and I'm not sure I want to know!

4. When I think about living as a gender variant person, my feelings are . . .

   a. Positive! I can't wait until I'm able to be myself. (Or: I feel like I can already be myself!)

   b. Neutral. I'm not sure if that label fits me.

   c. Negative. I don't think I want people to see me that way.

5. When I first met a gender variant person, I thought . . .

   a. That's me! Twinsies!

   b. I think we might share something in common, but I'm not sure.

   c. That's not me. I would never look or act like that.

If you answered **mostly a**: You're ready to jump head first into the larger community of gender variant people—or maybe you already have. Congratulations! Now that you're comfortable with this community, maybe your next step is organizing your own group, welcoming others into your existing group, or taking steps to make your community more inclusive.

If you answered **mostly b**: You worry about being accepted by other people. You might be worried that you're not gender variant "enough" or in the "right" way. Or you might not be sure you're part of the gender variant community or the larger queer community at all. Just remember it's okay to experiment with your identity, even if you end up deciding a certain identity isn't for you.

If you answered **mostly c**: You don't feel like you fit in right now. That's okay. There are a lot of possible causes for these feelings. Here are some reasons you might not feel part of your local queer or gender variant community:

1. You've accepted negative messages about gender variant people. Maybe you've picked up clues that the people around you think gender variant people are unattractive or abnormal social outcasts. This might make you less likely to want to think of yourself as part of that community.

2. There are important differences between you and the gender variant people in your community. If you're a cisgender person who is gender nonconforming, for example, you might have some things in common with trans people, but not everything. It's up to you to decide whether you can still give and receive support in that community or whether you need to find another group of people with identities closer to your own.

3. Your local community hasn't made an effort to welcome people like you. You might have found that some queer spaces in your area are dominated by people with certain identities. For example, your city might not have a support group for nonbinary people. Or maybe the only people who show up to your local queer hiking group are cisgender gay men. You may need to find other spaces to explore your identity. Or maybe it's time to flex those leadership muscles and start a group of your own.

4. You're not there yet. Maybe you're still not sure whether you belong. Maybe it's just too overwhelming at this point to interact with gender variant people when you still don't have your own identity figured out. Don't worry—your community will be waiting for you when you're ready.

EXERCISE: YOUR INNER CRITIC

Meet your inner critic—the little voice in your head that judges the things you do, say, and think. Have you ever told yourself unhelpful things like *you're going to fail* or *you shouldn't be feeling that way*? Then this exercise is for you.

Complete these sentences.

I feel positive about my gender identity when I think about _____,

but then I feel bad about myself when I remember _____.

I sometimes want to express myself with _____,

but then I tell myself I can't because _____.

I sometimes feel _____, but then I shut down that feeling by

telling myself _____.

Noticing what your inner critic is telling you can help you separate helpful thoughts from unhelpful ones. Instead of readily accepting your inner critic's harsh judgment, you can make your inner dialogue go in a different direction and silence your critic when you need to. Try talking back to your inner critic and challenging the judgments they're making about you and your thoughts.

EXERCISE: GREAT EXPECTATIONS

As you get older, the people around you will start to expect more of you. Some of these expectations are reasonable, like taking out the trash or driving safely. But others are based on stereotypes, like "acting ladylike" or "being the man of the house."

This journaling exercise will help you think about these expectations in a more critical way. Write responses to these questions:

What do people expect of me?

Which of these expectations are reasonable?

Which of these expectations seem unreasonable?

Trust your answers, and come back to them if you're ever feeling pressured.

_____

_____

_____

_____

_____

_____

_____

_____

_____

_____

EXERCISE: SLOW DOWN AND BREATHE

Some of the exercises in part 2 may have made you uncomfortable or anxious. That's normal—you're working through some big feelings. Let's pause and learn a technique called **slow breathing**.

6 breaths

60 seconds

Slow breathing is different from deep breathing or meditation. You don't have to worry about how deeply you're breathing, and you don't have to think about anything in particular. Just set a timer for two minutes. Take about six breaths per minute. (That's 10 seconds per full breath, if you haven't already done the math.) When you're finished, you should feel more relaxed—and hopefully ready to keep going.

That's it for part 2. In this section, you've gained greater knowledge about yourself, faced some tough situations, and taken a look at the bigger community of queer and gender variant people around you. Next, we're going to look at problems and scenarios you might run into in real life, and we'll brainstorm ways to solve them. On to part 3!

YOUR GENDER IDENTITY IN REAL LIFE: YOUR QUESTIONS ANSWERED

Welcome to the final part of this workbook. Here, we'll look at some scenarios you might face in real life. We're going to move away from the more mental part of your gender journey and toward the practical, real-world part: coming out, moving forward, and being your true self.

Exploring gender identity comes with a lot of questions. *How do I bring the super-secret-hidden-inside-me to the outside? How do I explain why I look different now? What do I do about sports, family, college, work? What if I get to the end of this workbook and I'm still not 100 percent sure about my gender identity?* Don't worry! Part 3 is going to help you think about the answers to these questions.

The format is Q&A. First, a real-world scenario that you might face in the future or might have already encountered will be presented. Then we'll talk about tips and ideas to deal with each scenario. We'll also use interactive exercises to work through the feelings that come up as you go through changes in life—not just gender transition or exploration but growing up, becoming more independent, and making decisions about your future.

Let's get started!

I HAVE A QUESTION ABOUT . . .

Q: I want to speak up when someone accidentally misgenders me, but I freeze up when it happens. How do I let someone know when they slip without making either of us uncomfortable?

A: Two things to remember. First, they're probably going to be grateful to you for speaking up. Most people don't want to accidentally misgender someone. Second, it doesn't have to be a big deal. You're not scolding them; you're giving them valuable information.

If they apologize briefly and move on, great. If they keep apologizing, it's okay to change the subject. What if they keep using the wrong pronouns? Don't feel bad about correcting them more than once. They'll eventually realize that it's important to you—or get tired of being corrected!

Try this exercise. Practice saying these lines in a mirror or to a friend:

→ "Oh, I actually use [pronouns], not [other pronouns]."

→ "I'm a [gender]. I go by [pronoun]."

→ "I'm actually going by [name] now."

→ "It's [pronoun]. No biggie."

→ "It would mean a lot to me if you try to remember that I'm [name] now."

Q: I hear people talking about having a "personal style." My clothes don't have a style! They're just . . . clothes. I want to wear clothes that fit my gender better, but I don't know what looks good on me. I end up buying stuff and never wearing it. How do I develop a style?

A: Have you ever made a moodboard? A moodboard is a collage of pictures, words, and ideas that express an idea, style, or feeling. You can create one online using sites like Pinterest or Canva or make one by hand by gluing or taping magazine photos, drawings, color samples, and fabric swatches to a sturdy piece of poster board or cardboard.

Go to an online clothing store or fashion site and see what catches your eye, or walk around the mall and take pictures of outfits in store windows. Scroll through Instagram and see what the celebrities and influencers you follow are wearing. Are there musicians or TV characters whose outfits you like? All of these can go on your moodboard.

Your moodboard samples don't have to be just pictures of clothes. Look through art and design magazines and see what colors and textures make you happy. Maybe you're into '70s styles or neutral colors. Do you love *The Nightmare Before Christmas*? Maybe you're a budding goth.

As you add more elements to your moodboard, you'll start seeing themes emerge. Try to put words to those themes. Maybe you'll find there's a fabric that you keep coming back to (animal prints?) or an era or style (grunge?) that shows up multiple times on your moodboard. Knowing how to describe your style will be the perfect jumping-off point to figuring out what to buy or trade with friends or family or how to repurpose stuff you already own.

Q: I've thought about dressing in a way that's truer to who I am, but I feel silly when I put on something different from what I normally wear. I want to go out of the house like this . . . but I don't . . . but I do! Will I ever be able to dress the way I really want to?

A: Baby steps! Trust me, it's going to get easier with practice.

You know how when people are afraid of snakes, they practice getting over their fear using pictures of snakes or rubber snakes? Well, you can practice wearing Shiny New Clothes without having to make the leap from Old Boring Clothes all at once. Wearing your favorite clothes in private is a good start, but getting out of the house might take some prep work.

Accessories can be a good way to practice making changes in your wardrobe. If a dress is too big a change, try a barrette or a bracelet. You can also change up one part of your wardrobe—for example, more masculine shirts or more feminine shoes. If you don't feel comfortable with a bold statement, try something more subtle, like wearing women's jeans instead of men's or vice versa. Different underwear or socks could be a fun "undercover" way to be yourself.

Want a bigger challenge? Wear your new clothes around strangers who don't know what you normally dress like. Try on a bra or wear those short-shorts you've been saving for a special occasion, and go somewhere new.

Here's another style exercise for you. What are some clothing items that express your gender identity but are so low-key you'd be okay wearing them now? Draw them in the box on the left on the following page. What's the most outrageous outfit you'd ever think of wearing—something you're totally not ready to wear now? Draw it in the box on the right. How do you get from left to right? Draw some clothing items in the middle box that aren't too scary to wear but aren't totally comfortable, either.

LOW-KEY	MIDDLE OF THE ROAD	OUTRAGEOUS

The clothing items in the middle are your "rubber snakes," in a way. These items will challenge your anxieties about expressing your identity but aren't going to freak you out *so* much that you stuff them in the back of your closet and forget about them. These things will help you get comfortable moving toward that amazing outfit on the right.

Q: There's a girl in my class I really like. But I don't think she knows I'm a trans guy. I started going to a new school this year, and I think people just assume I'm cis. If I decide to ask her on a date, when do I tell her I'm trans?

A: There aren't any set rules about this, so let your own comfort and safety be your guide. If you think you know her well enough now, you might feel comfortable telling her right away. If not, the first couple of dates are a good time to get a sense of whether someone is a safe person to come out to. Use your critical thinking skills. Do they seem like someone you can trust with your private information, or do they tell you other people's secrets? Do they seem LGBTQ-friendly in general?

Go on that first date or two, and if you aren't feeling comfortable, you can go your separate ways without anything being disclosed. But let's say you decide you'd like her to know about your gender history. Some people have these conversations somewhere public, like a coffee shop, especially if they're worried about their safety. Others want to keep things as private as possible. Either way, make sure you start by telling her how you'd like this information to be handled. If you're not out at school, make sure she knows not to out you without your permission.

Don't go into the conversation expecting that being trans is going to be a negative. For many people, finding out that a potential boyfriend is trans is neutral or positive information. That said, be prepared for a range of reactions, including rejection. As upsetting as this may be, if someone rejects you for being trans, they're probably not someone you want to date anyway.

Q: Just as those films in health class predicted, I'm going through puberty. I've been having mixed feelings about what's happening to my body. I've heard a lot of trans people say that they hated going through puberty, but for me, it's mostly just . . . strange. I feel good about some changes and bad about others. And sometimes I wish I could hide in my room until it's all over. Is this normal?

A: Watching your body change and grow in unpredictable ways is always going to be a weird experience, no matter whether you're gender variant or not. However, puberty can be especially challenging if there's a mismatch between these changes and your gender identity. You may struggle to reconcile your self-image with the way you look now. Discomfort with your body may create feelings of anger, sadness, numbness, or anxiety, and you might have the urge to hide your body or withdraw socially. But you might also feel positive or neutral about some changes—for example, you might be excited about getting taller, even if you have negative feelings about your chest. Getting mental health support from a therapist or school counselor is always a good idea, whatever your feelings about these changes.

Some gender variant youth receive medications to halt the effects of puberty, commonly called puberty blockers. These medications pause puberty-related changes in your body (though they don't reverse changes that have already happened) in order to give you time to come to a better understanding of your gender identity. You can stop taking these medications at any time and allow your body to go through puberty, or you can begin gender-affirming hormone therapy. A trans-competent primary care doctor will be able to help you decide whether puberty blockers are right for you. See page 18 for more information on where to find one.

Q: I got my first job bussing tables this summer. Yay! Except that someone I know from school accidentally outed me to my shift supervisor, and now she's making mean comments. When I asked her to stop, she said she'd go to the owner and have me fired. What do I do?

A: First off, know your rights! In 2020, the Supreme Court ruled that gender variant people in the United States are protected under the Civil Rights Act of 1964, which means that it's illegal to fire or refuse to hire someone for being gender variant or to treat them differently at work.

Now that you know what your supervisor is doing is illegal, speak to the owner and let them know the behavior needs to stop if that's safe and practical for you. Make it clear that your coworker treating you differently because you're trans is illegal workplace discrimination. If it doesn't stop, or if your boss retaliates against you in some way, you can make a complaint to your state's department of labor or human rights office or file a federal charge of discrimination with the Equal Employment Opportunity Commission (EEOC; see the resources section on page 110 for how to do this). You can also contact the Transgender Law Center or other legal help agencies (also in the resources section) if you need help figuring out your options.

Q: I've already come out to my immediate family, but I want to talk to my other relatives about my gender identity. I need to figure out how to use words they'll understand. I don't know if they've ever seen a trans person, even on TV! Some of them don't speak English as a first language. How do I tell them I'm a girl now?

A: Even if they're loving and supportive in other ways, sometimes it can be tough for family members to wrap their heads around big concepts like gender identity. You might want to start with simpler language if you know someone doesn't know much about gender identity, especially if your relative speaks English as a second language or if you have to translate phrases into a different language.

You may need to address some myths about trans people. For example, you may need to explain that being gender variant is different from being gay or lesbian, which is a common misunderstanding. In fact, in some languages, the words for *gay/lesbian*, *effeminate man/masculine woman*, *drag queen/king*, and *gender variant person* can be the same. Some people think that being gender variant automatically means you'll be making physical changes to your body or having surgery. You might want to think about what you're willing to discuss about these plans if your relatives ask.

Make sure you don't make assumptions based on a relative's age or general attitudes. I've had clients who thought Grandma was too old to understand what gender identity is or that a great uncle would automatically be prejudiced because he's "traditional," only to discover that family member became their biggest supporter.

It can be easier to understand gender identity if the information comes from a film or TV show. Your relatives might also be more likely to trust information that comes from authority figures, like mental health professionals and researchers. This is where documentaries and TV specials about gender identity can be helpful (see the resources section on page 111 for suggestions).

It might be useful to think about what you need from each relative. Why are you telling them in the first place? Do you need every relative to understand everything about your gender identity? Or do you just want them to accept your new name and use the right pronouns?

In other words, you may not need to get into a long, complicated explanation about your identity label. Maybe you just need to reassure your relatives that you're happier this way. Maybe you just need to talk about the basics for now.

Let's do a short exercise so you can start preparing to talk about your identity.

Think about the relatives you're close to. What do they need to know? Why do they need to know these things? In other words, what do you need them to *do*?

_____

_____

_____

What about the relatives you see only during the holidays? What do they need to know? Why?

_____

_____

_____

Come back to these lines and review them when you're ready to have those conversations.

Q: I just came out as genderfluid, and so far, the only genderfluid people I know are online. It's been fun getting to know people like me. But someone on Tumblr has been sending me creepy messages and stalking me on other sites. What do I do?

A: Here are a few tips for keeping yourself safe in online queer communities. I know, I'm an adult and you don't want a lecture from me. But take it from someone who has been on the internet since Windows 95: it can get a little weird out there.

→ If someone sends you messages that make you uncomfortable, block them and report them to the site administrators, even if you don't know if these messages are technically illegal or against the site rules. Don't worry about getting in trouble or hurting that person's feelings. Consider bringing in an adult you trust in your offline life if that's safe for you.

→ Sometimes, people might try to manipulate you into doing things that make you uncomfortable. If someone you meet online says something like "send me your photos or I'll hurt myself," don't hesitate to block them. You are not responsible for someone else's feelings, especially if that person is trying to make you do something you're not okay with.

→ Always be careful with people who try to test your boundaries or who do or say things you've asked them not to. If you feel uncomfortable saying no to someone, that's a sign that something has gone wrong.

→ If you choose to talk to adults online, remember that safe adults don't ask minors for help, money, intimate photographs or videos, or emotional support.

→ Don't engage with trolls. They'll only increase their efforts if they think they can make you angry. Block them and move on.

→ **Doxxing** is when someone uses info you've shared online to figure out who you really are. Have you ever posted a story online and then realized that it revealed details about your life, like the name of your school? Have you ever accidentally shared a photo of yourself with clues about where you live, like the front of your house? Make sure none of your posts accidentally provides information about who you are.

Q: My mom asked me the other day if I'll be able to have kids after I physically transition. The thing is, I don't know! I'm okay with adopting, but I also might decide that I want biological kids someday. But I also want surgery and hormone therapy. What are my options?

A: Ah, the grandkids question—a favorite of moms everywhere. The details of this answer are going to depend on whether you were assigned female at birth (AFAB) or assigned male at birth (AMAB) and what kinds of procedures you have. Your ability to have biological children may also depend on the specifics of your medical history and the conditions you may have.

Hormone therapy can decrease your fertility, though many people who have undergone hormone therapy have successfully had biological children. Some genital surgeries can make having biological children difficult or impossible (though surgery on your chest, face, or other parts won't have any effect on your fertility). Some gender variant people freeze their eggs or sperm before they undergo hormone therapy or surgery. Some use a surrogate and/or use donor eggs or sperm to help them have children. These things can be expensive, but some of them may be covered by health insurance.

Q: Being a Christian is a really important part of my life. But as I've started to figure out my gender, I'm finding that my identity and my beliefs seem to be in conflict. My pastor says people like me are "lost souls." I don't know what to think. How do I keep my faith without losing who I am?

A: If you're struggling with your beliefs, whatever your religion, you can start by asking yourself a few questions:

→ How did I come to believe that being gender variant was wrong? Is this a core belief of my religion or just something my religious leaders believe?

→ Is there another way to interpret these teachings? Are there religious scholars who don't think my religion condemns people like me?

→ Are there any faith communities within my religion that embrace gender variant people? Would I be welcome in those communities?

→ Would I feel comfortable staying in my faith community even if they did not fully accept my identity?

Many people of many different faiths have been able to find harmony between their beliefs and their identities and have been embraced by churches, temples, and mosques that welcome people of all genders. The resources section (page 110) lists sites where you can find religious perspectives on gender identity and learn about welcoming faith communities.

Q: My health class did a week of sex ed, but I still have more questions than answers. They talked only about sex between cis men and women, which doesn't apply to me. And they basically just told us not to have sex! My parents just say I need to have "safe sex" when I start having sex in the future. But what does safe sex mean for people with bodies like mine?

A: When we talk about making sex safer, we're really talking about two different things. The first is preventing pregnancy, also known as contraception. The second is avoiding sexually transmitted infections (STIs). These are diseases that a partner can give you during sex if they're infected.

Let's talk about STIs first. The best way of preventing STIs is by using a barrier: a thin layer of latex or other stretchy material between you and your partner that stops microorganisms from reaching you. Whenever one partner's genitals touch another partner's genitals or mouth, a barrier should be used. Barriers include internal condoms (a latex sheath that goes inside the vagina or anus), external condoms (a latex sheath that goes over the penis), and dental dams (a flat sheet of latex used for oral sex on someone with a vulva).

Another way of preventing STIs is by sticking to activities that don't involve your mouth or genitals touching your partner's mouth or genitals. Touching each other with your hands is a low-risk activity as long as you wash your hands between touching your partner's genitals and your own. Lube can make the experience more comfortable.

What about pregnancy? First, know that hormone therapy doesn't prevent you from getting pregnant if you're AFAB or getting someone pregnant if you're AMAB. An AFAB person can't get someone pregnant and an AMAB person can't get pregnant. Condoms are a cheap and effective way to prevent pregnancy during vaginal sex, which is the only way pregnancy can happen (not by anal sex, oral sex, or touching with hands).

There are other contraceptive methods that an AFAB person can get from a doctor. These may include a pill, a patch, a shot, or devices that get inserted or implanted into their body. None of these are 100 percent effective and none prevent STIs, so you should still use a condom.

Make sure you talk to your partner about what method you want to use before you have sex so you can take a trip to the doctor or pharmacy together. If you have sex without a barrier and you're worried you or your partner could be pregnant, you can get emergency contraception without a prescription at most pharmacies. The resources section (page 108) lists places you can get condoms, contraception, and safer sex information.

Q: My family is really supportive of my identity. Almost too supportive! There are, like, five articles about trans kids on the fridge right now. My parents want to sit in on my sessions with my therapist, even though I'm not sure I'm okay with that. They're always asking me what they can do to help. What can I tell them?

A: It sounds like you and your family aren't on the same page about how they can support you. When someone loves you, it can be hard for them to fight the urge to jump in and help before asking you what kind of help you actually need. And sometimes, what you need is *less help*.

Here's an activity to help you figure out what you need right now from your family. Put an X at a point along each line that best indicates what your family can do to support you. You can use this to get more clarity for yourself before discussing the matter with your family, or you can show this to your family as a jumping-off point for discussion.

I NEED YOU TO . . .

OFFER ME MORE HELP

⟷

LET ME MAKE MY OWN MISTAKES

ASK MORE QUESTIONS

⟷

ASK FEWER QUESTIONS

TELL THE WORLD

⟷

KEEP IT UNDER WRAPS

CELEBRATE MY UNIQUENESS

⟷

TREAT ME THE SAME AS EVER

BE MY CHAMPION

⟷

LET ME FIGHT MY BATTLES

OFFER ME INFO

⟷

LET ME FIND MY OWN INFO

GIVE YOUR OPINION

⟷

ASK IF I WANT YOUR OPINION

DISCUSS GENDER IN THE NEWS

⟷

GIVE ME A BREAK FROM THE NEWS

ASK ME FOR GENDER INFO

⟷

DO YOUR OWN RESEARCH

DO SOME THINGS FOR ME

⟷

SUPPORT MY INDEPENDENCE

SPEND TIME WITH ME

⟷

GIVE ME MORE SPACE

Q: The graduation committee asked for baby photos of all the graduating students. I identify as male, but in every one of my baby photos, I have a huge, frilly bow on my head. These photos are going to be projected onto a screen in the auditorium for everyone to see. What do I do?

A: A lot of gender variant teens have some variations of these questions:

→ What do I do if someone wants to see childhood photos of me (or if my parents insist on displaying those photos at home)?

→ Can I use the phrase "when I was a little girl" if I was outwardly a little boy?

→ I was in the Girl Scouts—can I substitute "Boy Scouts" when I explain where I learned to start a campfire?

Sometimes, people worry that they're lying when they talk about their past and they change some details, and we've all been taught that it's wrong to lie.

But you wouldn't be lying if you used a word like *boy* to describe your past self. You weren't any less a boy just because people didn't call you one. And you aren't hurting anyone by telling a little white lie to avoid having an uncomfortable conversation or outing yourself. So go ahead and use a baby photo of your brother or your dad from the family album if it makes you more comfortable.

Q: I'm a 17-year-old trans girl. I used to think I wanted to date only boys. After I started physically and socially transitioning, I started thinking more and more about dating girls. What does this mean?

A: Many gender variant people find that their attractions change or expand when they begin to get more comfortable in their own skin. Some people start to feel more attracted to different kinds of people because they feel more secure in their gender identity. Maybe it made you feel weird to think about dating girls before because you thought it made you less of a girl yourself. Some people's attractions shift because they feel more at home with their bodies. Maybe the thought of being with a girl triggered your dysphoria because of the contrast between your bodies, but it doesn't now that you've started your transition.

Both cis and gender variant people can have these kinds of shifts in their attractions, and it's hard to know exactly what causes them. Regardless, your sexual orientation doesn't say anything about your gender identity, so don't worry about that aspect.

Q: I hate talking about my body. Words like *breasts* make me cringe. Do I have to use these words? What other words can I use that might make me cringe less?

A: You don't have to use the same words your doctor uses to describe your body. As you said, it can make you feel a lot of dysphoria to have to use words that don't fit your gender identity. Some gender variant people are more comfortable with a different body part vocabulary. Here are some words you can use for the following parts of your body:

CONVENTIONAL WORD	ALTERNATIVE WORD
Penis	Clitoris, vulva, genitals, girl dick, parts, junk, bits
Testes	Labia, bits, junk
Vagina	Front hole, genitals, parts, junk
Breasts	Chest, torso, top
Clitoris	Penis, dick, genitals, parts, junk, bits

You don't just have to use these words to describe your own body. You can ask other people to use them, like anyone you choose to explore your sexuality with (if you do!) or medical professionals. It's one easy way to help you get to a better place with your body.

Q: I just started binding my chest to get a flatter look. Huge difference! But one of my friends said that binding can be unhealthy. Is that true?

Q: I'm AMAB and I want to start tucking so I can wear tight jeans without a bulge. Is there anything I should worry about?

A: You can do both of those things safely, but yes, there are ways to accidentally hurt yourself, and it's important to avoid doing that.

Let's talk about binding first. Some people wear binders made specifically for gender variant people. If you don't have access to a binder, a sports bra or athletic compression shirt is a safe alternative. Binding too tightly can make your back and chest hurt, restrict your breathing, or even lead to rib fractures, so make sure you use the correct size. Watch for signs like pain, numbness, tingling, or light-headedness, which can indicate that you're binding too tightly. Make sure to keep both your binder and your skin clean to prevent irritation and infections. Never use Ace bandages or duct tape. These materials can damage your skin, constrict your breathing, and lead to rib fractures. Taking a day off, if that's possible for you, can reduce the risks of binding.

Tucking can be done safely using something called a gaff: a tight pair of underwear designed for tucking. You can also use medical tape or a tight pair of regular underwear—but don't use duct tape! (Rule of thumb: duct tape should *never* go on your body.) Tucking shouldn't hurt. If anything starts hurting, stop! Otherwise, there aren't any known negative effects of tucking. So tuck away.

Q: I'm usually a happy person, but watching the news gives me anxiety. Sometimes I'm afraid that I'm going to wake up tomorrow and my rights are going to be gone. I know there's been a lot of progress for gender variant people, but there's also a lot of hate out there. How do I get past my fears?

A: You're right. Everything's not all right in the world. But let me give you some personal perspective.

In the 15 years that I've been an out, proud trans man, I have seen changes that I never would have thought possible when I was a teen. I've seen trans rights go from the margins to the forefront of the LGBTQ movement. I've witnessed many federal court rulings that have affirmed the rights of gender variant people and the larger LGBTQ community to work, live, and love. Today is not perfect, but it's better than yesterday. Anytime I've ever felt hopeless about gender rights, I've been proven wrong.

This didn't happen by accident. It's the result of the work of activists throughout the last century who have stood up to violence and ridicule for the right to exist as gender variant people. It's important to speak up when things aren't right. I'm not going to say everything's all right now, but it's important to recognize how far we've come and how many sacrifices the generations before us have made.

Activism and organizing might be the key to feeling better about the future. It's empowering to feel like you're not just sitting on the sidelines, even if you take only a small and simple action, like posting gender positivity on your social media or speaking up when you hear someone say something intolerant. You can be the kind of role model that younger gender variant people look up to. As you get older and flex your activist muscles, you might be the person who ends up making a huge difference for gender variant people in the future.

Q: Ever since I started presenting as male at school, I keep getting picked on. People in the hallway call me names or bump into me on purpose. My teachers won't help, even during the rare times it happens in front of them. One teacher told me to stand up for myself. Another told me to ignore it. A third teacher said I was drawing too much attention to myself by dressing the way I do. What should I do?

A: Sometimes, adults will tell you it's your job to address bullying on your own. This advice often comes from a well-meaning place: After all, isn't being assertive a good idea? Sure, but telling you to solve the problem yourself places the entire responsibility of preventing bullying on the victim. Being bullied isn't the result of *your* actions, and most bullies won't stop just because you told them to. In some cases, "standing up for yourself" may even put you in danger.

Bullying happens when schools don't act to address it and there aren't any consequences for students who mistreat other students. With this in mind, you or your parents may want to speak to your school principal to discuss how they plan to keep you safe at school. This may include actions like enforcing consequences for bullying, monitoring hallways and stairwells, and training teachers to stop bullying behavior when they see it.

If your principal doesn't take you seriously, it might be time to escalate the matter to your school district's superintendent (an administrator who is in charge of all of the schools in a district) or Title IX coordinator (a legally required staff member in every school district that receives federal funding whose job it is to investigate sex discrimination, which includes mistreatment of gender variant students). You can also file a complaint with your state's department of education or the US Department of Education. Turn to the resources section (page 110) to find out how or to read up on your rights as a student.

Q: I got into an argument with my sister and she said something awful and transphobic to me. I'm SUPER mad at her. But as angry as I am, I don't want this to be the end of our relationship. How should I handle it?

A: Siblings, right? They can make you dream about life as an only child.

Before flying off the handle completely, try a breathing exercise to calm down. Trace your finger clockwise around the square, starting on the left. Breathe in and out, following the instructions.

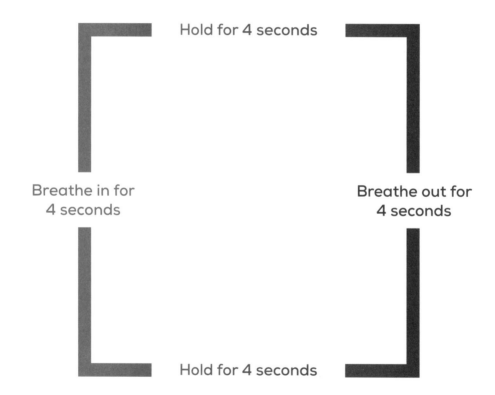

Hold for 4 seconds

Breathe in for
4 seconds

Breathe out for
4 seconds

Hold for 4 seconds

After you've calmed down, think about what you need from your sibling. Maybe you need them to apologize or use different language. Or maybe you just need them to give you some space. Use this exercise to think about what you need. You can use it to help you keep a clear head during discussions with siblings, friends, or other people who make you angry.

It hurts me when you . . .

_____

_____

_____

_____

_____

_____

What I need from you right now is . . .

_____

_____

_____

_____

_____

_____

I don't want to fight with you. I want us to be able to . . .

_____

_____

_____

_____

_____

_____

Q: I started running last year under my old name, when I was still known as Grace. Now that I'm out as a boy and have been taking testosterone for the last few weeks, is it still okay to run in local 5Ks? What are the rules for trans athletes?

A: You can be just as great an athlete after you transition. The way you can compete depends on *how* you've transitioned. The rules are different depending on where you live and what kinds of competitions you enter, but most athletic federations (including the NCAA and the Olympics) follow the standards set by the World Anti-Doping Agency (WADA), a foundation started by the International Olympic Committee to make sure that all athletes have a level playing field.

These guidelines say that AFAB athletes who have not had hormone therapy can compete in either the male or female division of their sport. However, if you're AFAB and you start taking testosterone, you have to start competing in the male division of your sport because testosterone gives you a competitive advantage. So you *can* check "M" on your entry form even if you haven't started hormone therapy, but once you do start, you *have* to check "M." An AMAB athlete can compete in the female division of their sport only after one year of hormone therapy. This is to make sure that AMAB athletes have the same (lower) level of testosterone as other female participants.

None of these guidelines say anything about how you have to identify your gender. You can compete in the female division of your sport and still identify as male or nonbinary, for example, and you can always use the name and pronouns of your choice. (It may also be worth it to ask competition organizers if you can be identified with your preferred gender marker and pronouns during the competition, even if you're not competing in the division of that gender.) Having surgery won't affect your eligibility under these guidelines.

Basically, the rules are in place to make sure no one has an unfair advantage—not to police what pronouns you use or clothes you wear. These rules aren't perfect and can sometimes lead to gender variant athletes' bodies and medical decisions being scrutinized more than those of cisgender athletes or to athletes whose appearance isn't gender typical being accused of cheating. My advice is to keep advocating for yourself and being visible in your sport—you might end up making a big difference to future athletes like you.

Q: I need to come up with a new name—stat! I've picked a few, but I always end up changing my mind. How do I decide how to choose one?

A: So many options!

This name game should put you on the right track. In this exercise, you're not going to pick just one name—you're going to pick a lot of them. Maybe none of them will become the name you finally choose, but this will get you started on thinking about the kinds of names you like. Knowing what things you like about a name will help you narrow down your choices to a single name that has everything you're looking for.

Do you have a favorite letter? Maybe you're drawn to B names like Brian or Brandon. Pick some names that start with your favorite letter.

_____

_____

_____

How about your favorite time in history? Maybe you love the '20s and you're a Betty, Louise, or Ruby. Pick some names that remind you of a different time.

_____

_____

_____

Your favorite books might have suggestions for you. Are you an Alanna from the Song of the Lioness series or a James from *James and the Giant Peach*? Write down some names from books you love.

_____

_____

_____

Do you like names with the same initial as your birth name or variations of that name? Add a letter or drop a letter and see how it sounds.

_____

_____

_____

_____

Think of some names that remind you of places you've visited or places you'd like to go. Think Paris, Brooklyn, Walden, Sydney, or Acadia.

_____

_____

_____

_____

Q: I'm transfeminine, and I've been on hormone therapy for the last few months. It's not having the effects I want. Specifically, I really want to be curvy! I've heard that some transfeminine people inject their hips, butts, and boobs with silicone. Is this safe?

A: Injecting your body with silicone—or "pumping," as some people call it—is extremely dangerous. It's not the same as getting breast or butt implants. Silicone implants have a "shell" that prevents the silicone inside from moving around. They're usually implanted by trained medical professionals.

Reputable medical doctors don't do silicone injections because of the risks. These injections are usually performed by untrained people, often at "pumping parties" rather than medical facilities. The type of silicone that "pumpers" use isn't the type that doctors use for implants—it's the kind a plumber might use to caulk a bathtub. It's not sterile, and it can move around your body and cause bad things to happen, including infections and pulmonary embolisms (blocked arteries in your lungs). Instead of having the body you want, you could be permanently disfigured or even die.

So, don't seek out pumping if you want a curvier body. Instead, find a trans-aware primary care doctor, and talk to your doctor about how you can get the look you want. If you're on hormone therapy, it might just be a matter of waiting for the fat in your body to increase in different areas. Sometimes, hip and butt padding can help. If none of these things work for you, surgery can also help—but it should be performed by a medical doctor only.

Q: I'm nonbinary, and I plan to spend some time outdoors this summer. Last year's gear doesn't seem like it fits my gender anymore. I'd be a lot more comfortable in athletic gear and swimwear that doesn't gender me as male or female. Where can I find it?

A: If you're looking for swimwear and sportswear specifically for people who don't conform to gender norms, clothing companies like Outplay, Chromat, and Hirsuit can hook you up with gender-neutral gear. Companies like these offer active clothing with androgynous, body-inclusive looks (check the resources section on page 109). But even if you don't have access to such clothing, you should be able to find a style you like at any sportswear store or a range of online retailers.

If you tend to want to cover up, there are a lot of options for comfort and privacy. At the beach, you could try putting on a pair of board shorts, a sarong, or a beach dress. If you want to cover up your chest, buy a rash guard shirt (also known as a swim shirt). When you're playing sports, you can choose to go with full-length yoga pants, track pants, basketball shorts, or a sports skirt, depending on the activity. Long-sleeved tees can be worn in any season—in fact, a lot of people wear them for sun protection. Synthetic fabrics tend to be more breathable, so choose them over cotton whenever possible.

Maybe you're someone who likes to show off a little. If that's the case, you might want to mix and match from the men's and women's sections. At the beach, this might look like a tank top with board shorts, or a swim shirt and a bikini bottom. For sports, you could combine a tank top with bike shorts, split shorts, or running tights.

Whatever your style, make sure that you can move around comfortably. If you find that you can't move with complete freedom, you might want to find a friend who can sew (or learn yourself) so you can alter your clothes. Enjoy that outdoors time!

Q: I have to keep my gender exploration secret for now because I know my family isn't going to be okay with it. How do I explore my gender when I can't come out?

A: Hiding your identity is no fun, but there are ways you can explore and express your gender identity even when you're keeping it under wraps. Here's a short checklist of activities that might help you hold on to a sense of who you are.

☐ *Your body:* Can you make yourself more comfortable in it, even if it's just in private? For example, could you shave your legs, paint your nails, or put on something that makes your chest flatter?

☐ *Your face:* Can you wear makeup when your family isn't home? Could you temporarily draw on some facial hair with an eyeliner pencil? Can you use filters on your phone that make you look the way you'd like to look?

☐ *Your hair:* Can you use hair products (or even plain water) to style it in a way that makes you feel better about yourself, even if it's not the length or style you want?

☐ *Your clothes:* Do you feel safe having a secret stash of clothes that fit your gender identity? Can you dress in a gender-affirming way in private? Do you have the option of wearing a small piece of gender-affirming clothing under your regular clothes? Are there types of clothing that fit your gender assigned at birth but look more feminine, masculine, or androgynous?

☐ *Your persona:* Can you make your online presence gender affirming? Could you use your chosen name and pronouns on the internet? Is there someone you could come out to who could affirm your gender?

☐ *Your truth:* Can you create a small space in your room that holds the truth of your gender, even if it's just in the back of your closet, your diary, or a secret box tucked away somewhere?

Q: This is the last Q&A exercise. Can I write my own?

A: You sure can. Think of a question you've always had about yourself. It could be about your gender identity, your past, your future, or anything else. Write it down.

_____

_____

_____

_____

You can come back to this question anytime. It might be a month, a year, or even a decade from now. Maybe you'll have answered it by then. Or maybe you'll have dozens more questions to add to it. The wonderful part of gender exploration is knowing that you'll never run out of questions.

KEEP EXPLORING, KEEP QUESTIONING, AND KEEP BEING YOU!

You've reached the end of the gender exploration exercises in this workbook. But this isn't the end of your gender exploration. Feel free to flip back through your answers and review them, add to them, or reflect on how your feelings have changed as you've progressed.

You've answered a lot of questions about yourself, but the most important ones are still ahead of you. What will you do with your newfound self-awareness? What does your knowledge about the big, beautiful, sparkling person inside you mean to your future? How will you use the words you've written in these pages to become the person you've always wanted to be or to change the world for the people who come after you? The answers to these questions lie ahead of you. Keep growing, get moving, and don't stop learning about yourself!

MOVING FORWARD

Just by making your way through this workbook, you've committed a brave act. Being willing to think deeply about your gender identity and answer tough questions means you're strong enough to face truths about yourself that could be scary or confusing. But it also means you have enough faith in your innermost feelings about yourself that you're willing to deal with uncertainty and doubt for the chance to create a better future.

It's possible you don't feel certain about your gender identity just yet. Maybe you're even less certain of your gender identity than when you opened this workbook. That's normal. If there's one truth we've confronted together, it's that you don't have to reach a definite conclusion about your gender right away. Your feelings about your identity are valid right now, whether or not they take the form of an identity label or change in the future.

However, it's also possible that you're much closer to figuring out your identity than you were when you started. Even if you aren't, you've accomplished a lot. You've worked on your personal boundaries, explored dating and sex, considered your personal style, and given some thought to who you want to be in the future. That's quite a journey. You have a long way to go, but I hope this workbook has been a helpful guide to the great things that lie ahead for you.

RESOURCES FOR TEENS

Support and General Resources

Many states, regions, and cities have local organizations that offer support for gender variant youth, and not all of them are listed in directories or resource guides. You can usually find them by Googling the name of your state or city along with words like *trans resources*, *trans support*, *trans group*, or *trans organization*. Meetup.com can also be a good place to find local groups and events.

The Transgender Teen Survival Guide (TransgenderTeenSurvivalGuide.tumblr.com) is a long-running blog and resource guide that offers a large number of guides, tips, and resource links. The blog's writers often answer questions submitted by teens.

The book *Trans Bodies, Trans Selves* is an excellent, comprehensive resource on trans life, including transition, health and mental health, relationships, sexuality, religion, trans history, and many other topics.

Crisis resources can be found in the sidebar on page 18 ("It Never Hurts to Ask for Help").

Trans Healthcare Providers

Information on finding a trans-friendly therapist or healthcare provider can be found in the sidebar on page 18 ("It Never Hurts to Ask for Help").

Sexuality Information

Up-to-date, gender inclusive information about sexuality can be found at:

→ Go Ask Alice (GoAskAlice.columbia.edu)

→ Scarleteen (Scarleteen.com)

→ Planned Parenthood (PlannedParenthood.org)

Planned Parenthood provides many free or affordable services related to trans healthcare and sexual and reproductive health. You can call 1-800-230-PLAN or visit PlannedParenthood.org/health-center to find your local health center.

ID Documents

Different states have different requirements for name changes, and some documents—like your passport or Social Security card—must be changed with federal agencies. The National Center for Transgender Equality provides a helpful tool to figure out your state's laws and the procedures for changing your gender on your ID; go to transequality .org/documents.

Swimwear, Sportswear, Clothing, and Undergarments

→   Outplay (OutplayBrand.com), Chromat (Chromat.co), Hirsuit (Hirsuit.co), and Rebirth Garments (RebirthGarments.com) sell swimwear and sportswear for all genders.

→   High-quality binders can be purchased from GC2B (gc2b.co), FLAVNT (FLAVNT.com), and Shapeshifters (Shapeshifters.co). Point of Pride (PointOfPride.org/chest-binder-donations) provides free binders and other gear to people who cannot afford or safely obtain them. In Canada, Gender Gear (GenderGear.ca/products) offers a binder recycling program that pro-vides pre-owned binders for $5.

→   Transguy Supply (TransguySupply.com) offers a variety of transmasculine products, such as packers and packing underwear.

→   Trans Tool Shed (TransToolShed.com) offers many products for both transfeminine and transmasculine people, including breast prosthetics, pocket bras, tucking underwear and supplies, shapewear, binders, packers/ harnesses, stand-to-pee devices, clothing, and books.

→   Undergarments and prosthetics for transfeminine people can also be found at Origami Customs (OrigamiCustoms.com/collections/all-transfemme) and En Femme (EnFemmeStyle.com). (Note: Unlike Origami, En Femme is not a trans-owned business; the site also sells products targeted toward cross-dressers, drag queens, and other people whose identities do not neces-sarily intersect with the trans community.) Point of Pride (PointOfPride.org /trans-femme-shapewear) collaborates with Origami Customs to offer free shapewear for transfeminine people who cannot afford or safely obtain it.

→   Tips on tucking can be found at PrideInPractice.org/articles /transgender-genital-tucking-guide.

→ A guide to finding tall and plus-size women's clothing and shoes at major retailers can be found at TransgenderMap.com/social/tall-clothing.

→ National clothing, underwear, and makeup stores with trans-friendly policies and trans-inclusive or gender-neutral fitting rooms include Target, Macy's, American Eagle/Aerie, Gap Inc. brands (which include Old Navy, Banana Republic, and Athleta), Abercrombie & Fitch, Sephora, Lush, and MAC.

→ Many products created by and for gender variant people can be found by searching sites that sell handmade products, such as Etsy.com.

Discrimination at School or Work

→ If you are facing discrimination at school, you can file a complaint with the US Department of Education at this site: ed.gov/about/offices/list/ocr /complaintintro.html. The National Center for Transgender Equality has information about your rights at school and actions to take if you face discrimination at transequality.org/know-your-rights/schools.

→ If you experience workplace discrimination, you can file a charge with the US Equal Employment Opportunity Commission (EEOC) at EEOC.gov /filing-charge-discrimination. You may also file with your state or local government (which may offer more protections) instead. The state agencies charged with enforcing these laws are called Fair Employment Practices Agencies (FEPAs); you can usually find your local FEPA by Googling "[your state or city] employment discrimination." The National Center for Transgender Equality (TransEquality.org) has information about your rights at work as well.

→ The Transgender Law Center (TransgenderLawCenter.org) and the Sylvia Rivera Law Project (SRLP.org) can provide assistance, referrals, and resources to people experiencing gender identity–related legal issues.

Religious Resources

→ The organization Gay Church (GayChurch.org) maintains a directory of LGBTQ-affirming Christian churches searchable by address at gaychurch .org/find_a_church. Queer Theology (QueerTheology.com) is a website with resources to help LGBTQ Christians embrace their sexuality and gender identity. Their resources on trans identity and Christian theology can be found at QueerTheology.com/transgender.

→ Advocates for Youth (AdvocatesForYouth.org) has produced a guide for young Muslims who are questioning their gender called "I'm a Muslim and My Gender Doesn't Fit Me: Resources for Trans Muslim Youth." It's available at AdvocatesForYouth.org/wp-content/uploads/2019/05/Im-Muslim-My-Gender-Doesnt-Fit-Me.pdf.

→ Eshel (EshelOnline.org) is an organization in New York City that provides support to Orthodox Jewish LGBTQ people. They maintain a warmline at 1-724-374-3501. Keshet (KeshetOnline.org) is an organization that promotes LGBTQ equality in the Jewish community and offers resources and events. TransTorah.org is a site about Jewish texts and traditions that speak to the gender variant experience. Congregation Beit Simchat Torah is a welcoming synagogue in New York that maintains a resource page for transgender Jews at CBST.org/transjews. Other resources can be found at PFLAG.org/jewish.

Gender Identity in Media

Here is a short list of documentaries, podcasts, and TV specials about gender variant identities in order of year. Although there are many films about people in the gender variant community, this list was chosen specifically to highlight positive, accurate, uplifting portrayals and the media achievements of gender variant people. (Content warning: Though all of these works are appropriate for teens, some deal with sexuality, medical treatment, discrimination, hate crimes, death, and other sensitive topics.)

→ *Paris Is Burning* (1990) follows the lives of Black and Latino trans and gay members of New York City's ballroom culture.

→ *Southern Comfort* (2001) tells the story of Robert Eads, a trans man dying of ovarian cancer who is determined to make one last appearance at a large transgender gathering in the deep South.

→ *Just Call Me Kade* (2002) is a documentary about a trans teen whose family embraces his identity.

→ *True Trans* (2014) tells the story of trans singer Laura Jane Grace of punk band Against Me!

→ *I Am Jazz* (2015–) is a TV series that follows the life of Jazz Jennings, a transgender teen girl.

→ *Becoming More Visible* (2016) showcases the experiences of four trans youth.

→ *We Exist: Beyond the Binary* (2018) is a documentary about nonbinary life that tells the story of Lauren, a nonbinary adult in their twenties, and features other nonbinary people and doctors who work with gender variant people.

→ *Science VS*: "The Science of Being Transgender" (2018) is a podcast episode in Gimlet Media's *Science VS* series about research on trans identities. It features two psychologists and an endocrinologist. You can listen to it for free at GimletMedia.com/shows/science-vs/j4hl23.

→ *Born to Be* (2019) is a documentary about the work of surgeon Dr. Jess Ting and other clinicians at the Mount Sinai Center for Transgender Medicine and Surgery.

→ *Disclosure: Trans Lives on Screen* (2020) is a documentary made by and starring trans and nonbinary people about how Hollywood presents gender variant people in film.

Gender Identity in Books and Graphic Novels

Here is a short list of books and graphic novels that speak to issues about gender identity and gender variance told from a wide variety of perspectives.

→ *Gender Queer* by Maia Kobabe

→ *Sorted* by Jackson Bird

→ *Sissy* by Jacob Tobia

→ *She's Not There* by Jennifer Finney Boylan

→ *Spellbound* by Bishakh Som

→ *The Prince and the Dressmaker* by Jen Wang

→ *The Witch Boy* by Molly Knox Ostertag

→ The *Dreadnought* series by April Daniels

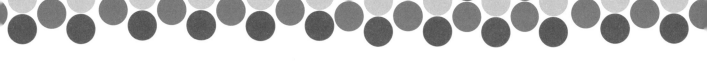

RESOURCES FOR PARENTS

If you're a parent of a teen who is questioning their gender identity, you may be wondering how to support your child or have questions about what your child's gender identity means to them. These resources can help you offer support and guidance.

→ Gender Spectrum (GenderSpectrum.org) provides a wide variety of resources and information for family members looking to learn more about gender identity and provide a supportive environment for their children.

→ PFLAG (PFLAG.org) is an organization with more than 400 local chapters that provides support to families with LGBTQ children, including support groups. You can find your local chapter at PFLAG.org/find-a-chapter.

→ My Kid Is Gay (MyKidIsGay.com) has resources and support for parents of LGBTQ kids and includes many resources for parents of gender variant kids, including those with nonbinary identities.

→ If you're struggling to understand gender identity and what it means for your child, check out the National Center for Transgender Equality's "About Transgender People" information hub at transequality.org/about-transgender.

REFERENCES

Bakker, Julie. "Brain Structure and Function in Gender Dysphoria." *Endocrine Abstracts* 56 (2018). doi.org/10.1530/endoabs.56.s30.3.

Bockting, Walter, Eli Coleman, Madeline B. Deutsch, Antonio Guillamon, Ilan Meyer, Walter Meyer III, Sari Reisner, Jae Sevelius, and Randi Ettner. "Adult Development and Quality of Life of Transgender and Gender Nonconforming People." *Current Opinion in Endocrinology, Diabetes and Obesity* 23, no. 2 (April 2016): 188–97. doi.org/10.1097/med.0000000000000232.

Bränström, Richard, and John E. Pachankis. "Reduction in Mental Health Treatment Utilization among Transgender Individuals after Gender-Affirming Surgeries: A Total Population Study." *The American Journal of Psychiatry* 177, no. 8 (August 2020): 727–34. doi.org/10.1176/appi.ajp.2019.19010080.

De Vries, Annelou L. C., Jenifer K. McGuire, Thomas D. Steensma, Eva C. F. Wagenaar, Theo A. H. Doreleijers, and Peggy T. Cohen-Kettenis. "Young Adult Psychological Outcome after Puberty Suppression and Gender Reassignment." *Pediatrics* 134, no. 4 (October 2014): 696–704. doi.org/10.1542/peds.2013-2958.

Dhejne, Cecilia, Roy Van Vlerken, Gunter Heylens, and Jon Arcelus. "Mental Health and Gender Dysphoria: A Review of the Literature." *International Review of Psychiatry* 28, no. 1 (2016): 44–57. doi.org/10.3109/09540261.2015.1115753.

Guillamon, Antonio, Carme Junque, and Esther Gómez-Gil. "A Review of the Status of Brain Structure Research in Transsexualism." *Archives of Sexual Behavior* 45 (2016): 1615–48. doi.org/10.1007/s10508-016-0768-5.

Neyt, Jennifer. "An Exclusive Interview with Oslo Grace." *Vogue Paris*, February 8, 2019. vogue.fr/fashion/article/an-exclusive-interview-with-oslo-grace.

Olson, Kristina R., Lily Durwood, Madeleine DeMeules, and Katie A. McLaughlin. "Mental Health of Transgender Children Who Are Supported in Their Identities." *Pediatrics* 137, no. 3 (March 2016). doi.org/10.1542/peds.2015-3223.

Peitzmeier, Sarah, Ivy Gardner, Jamie Weinand, Alexandra Corbet, and Kimberlynn Acevedo. "Health Impact of Chest Binding among Transgender Adults: A Community-Engaged, Cross-Sectional Study." *Culture, Health & Sexuality* 19, no. 1 (2017): 64–75. doi.org/10.1080/13691058.2016.1191675.

Ristori, Jiska, Carlotta Cocchetti, Alessia Romani, Francesca Mazzoli, Linda Vignozzi, Mario Maggi, and Alessandra Daphne Fisher. "Brain Sex Differences Related to Gender Identity Development: Genes or Hormones?" *International Journal of Molecular Sciences* 21, no. 6 (2020): 2123. doi.org/10.3390/ijms21062123.

Van de Grift, Tim C., Garry L. S. Pigot, Siham Boudhan, Lian Elfering, Baudewijntje P. C. Kreukels, Luk A. C. L. Gijs, Marlon E. Buncamper, et al. "A Longitudinal Study of Motivations before and Psychosexual Outcomes after Genital Gender-Confirming Surgery in Transmen." *The Journal of Sexual Medicine* 14, no. 12 (December 2017): 1621–28. doi.org/10.1016/j.jsxm.2017.10.064.

Weinforth, Géraldine, Richard Fakin, Pietro Giovanoli, and David Garcia Nuñez. "Quality of Life Following Male-to-Female Sex Reassignment Surgery." *Deutsches Ärzteblatt International* 116, no. 15 (2019): 253–60. doi.org/10.3238/arztebl.2019.0253.

Wilson, Erin C., Yea-Hung Chen, Sean Arayasirikul, H. Fisher Raymond, and Willi McFarland. "The Impact of Discrimination on the Mental Health of Trans*Female Youth and the Protective Effect of Parental Support." *AIDS and Behavior* 20 (2016): 2203–11. doi.org/10.1007/s10461-016-1409-7.

INDEX

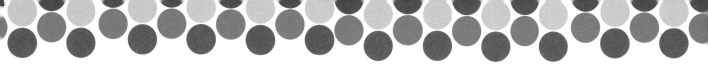

ABOUT THE AUTHOR

Andrew Maxwell Triska, LCSW, is a psychotherapist whose work focuses on gender identity and sexuality. Originally from Oregon and now based in New York, he is the author of multiple books and other written work on LGBTQ mental health topics and provides training and consulting on gender identity for organizations and businesses. He can be found on the internet at AndrewTriska.com.